The Quest for Spiritual Maturity

by

Tom Seals

ISBN 10:1-58427-275-9

ISBN 13: 978-158427-275-5

Tom Seals
College of Bible & Ministry
Lipscomb University
One University Park Drive
Nashville, Tennessee 37204

Table of Contents

Preface

We live in a world that inherently and consistently involves pressures, pressures that tend to diminish many important facets of our true selves, and with them our spiritual growth. Such pressures often overpower and defeat us spiritually resulting in lives far less effective than they potentially can be. Yet, if spirituality really matters to us, then in spite of such obstacles, we maintain a deep desire to grow and develop toward acceptability and likeness to Christ. We want the Christian faith to be a deeply-embedded part of our life, not just something casual, some surface affair. How do we achieve such a lifestyle? How do we develop into spiritually mature men and women of God in the face of the many persistent and powerful challenges of modernity?

It is such thoughts as these that motivated the writing of this book, *The Quest for Spiritual Maturity*. It is my prayer that every individual may be aided in his or her quest for spiritual growth through reading and applying the various principles examined and enjoined in this book. If one person is led to a closer relationship with God and Christ as a result of this study, the book will have achieved its intended purpose and will have been well worth the many hours spent in its preparation.

I am indebted to many for their assistance in this endeavor. I wish especially to thank my wife, Barbara, for patiently enduring the many hours spent away from her in preparing this book. I am also indebted to many writers of previous books on this subject matter, in particular those who greatly influenced my thinking as I have studied and reflected upon this issue through the years. A special note of appreciation is extended to Dr. Dan King, long-time friend and biblical scholar, for his careful reading of and helpful advice in the completion of this work. Finally, I thank my friend and fellow colleague, Leland Dugger, for the generous gift of his time and considerable talent in typing the manuscript. The positions taken and the views expressed are my own, but without these valuable associates, this work would not be a reality.

T.L.S.

Introduction

A great majority of us, if not all of us, recall having made this good confession: "I believe that Jesus is the Christ, the Son of the living God." This confession is a statement of belief that revealed a personal, whole-hearted, and sincere conviction which grew out of a decision to make a full and unreserved consecration of our lives to God. Following this confession we sealed our commitment through obedience to the command from the apostle Peter: "Repent, and be baptized...in the name of Jesus Christ for the forgiveness of your sins; and you shall receive the gift of the Holy Spirit" (Acts 2:38). At that moment we were united with Christ (cf. Gal. 3:27), released from bondage to the power and prince of this world, and ushered into the household of God. We then moved out into the world with the intent of becoming a living testimonial to the saving grace and model of spiritual perfection found in Jesus Christ, a leavening in-fluence upon our neighbors and friends, and a light shining in the darkness of this world.

Several years may have passed since we first took these challeng-ing steps of personal spiritual commitment. Due to the simple pass-ing of time, as well as various other erosive factors, there is a great likelihood that we may have arrived at a situation in life where we have come to an uneasy awareness that we may not have realized the high goals originally set forth at the time of our conversion to Christ. If so, this may be the time to frankly and openly encounter two very important possibilities: First, is it possible that our personal faith does not have the power and reality in our lives that it used to have or that it should have? We may still possess a great love for the ethical teaching of the Christian faith and the impressive figure of Jesus Christ. However, the spiritual aspects of the faith (worship, prayer, singing, and involvement), may just not be that appealing and inspiring to us anymore. Second, although I believe in the New Testament church and the Bible as the Word of God, it may seem that life is relatively lacking in that dynamic spirituality which the scriptures so clearly say should be developing and maturing in the life of a disciple of Christ who is indwelt by his Spirit. What has happened in my life after I first became a Christian? Have I missed something? Where is the growth and spirituality? Has anything really changed, or am I essentially the person I was before my conversion?

If the descriptions given above are genuinely indicative of what many of us are experiencing (and I am convinced that is what many of us do feel), then it may be that there is a solvable problem here. Our personal situation may fit into a rather ordinary and entirely repairable scenario. We have been taught all the orthodox doctrinal aspects of the Christian faith but it is very possible that we do not know about the reality of the finished work of Christ in the life of the newly born believer and what that ought to mean in our own personal lives. In relation to the reality which surrounds and concerns us in daily life, Christianity as presented in the classroom and from the pulpit often seems so utterly foreign, so completely alien, so far afield from where we really are at this moment in our lives. Many of us have actually become accustomed to living in two different and mutually exclusive spheres, the sphere of the church and the sphere of the world. We have even developed two languages to describe our different experiences, the special parochial language of the church and the so-called real language of the world around us.

It is with these thoughts in mind that it may be helpful for us to go back and spend a little time reviewing the reasons why we became Christians in the first place. Please bear in mind, though, that this review will prove both a necessary and a hazardous undertaking. It is necessary because we all desire to have our lives grounded on a sure and firm footing in the spiritual realm. But it is also a hazardous undertaking because we are focusing on an area of life which greatly concerns and affects our total outlook on life. This area of investigation pertains to man in the very essence of his being as man. Genuine, open, honest, and expectant[1] questioning such as

---

[1] We use the term "expectant" because in this quest, as in any quest, one gets from it what is put into it and what is expected from it.

this is something rare and really special. It may very well make a few extraordinary demands on those of us who are familiar with traditional Christianity. We will experience the power there is in stubborn clinging to self, and we will experience the strength of resistance to change that resides so deeply within each of us. We must, however, face these challenges if we are ever to become the kind of disciples of Christ that we are meant to be and that we hope to be. If in matters pertaining to the spiritual aspect we do not grow out of those ideas that we entertained during childhood, then our ideas will remain perennially childish and immature. Such checks in Christian growth are remarkably dangerous because they almost inescapably lead to the unfortunate and undesirable separation of faith from understanding. As Paul says so well, "Brethren, do not be children in your thinking; be babes in evil, but in thinking be mature" (1 Cor. 14:20; cf. Heb. 6:1-3). We must move on toward spiritual maturity. If we do not move on, we inevitably and inexorably go back; there is no standing still. It may be comfortable and seemingly secure to maintain one's life in a state of equilibrium by residing in the elementary stages of the faith, but we are convinced beyond all doubt that such is the way of an immature and stagnant spiritual life.

It is the conviction of this author that the Christian faith remains a vital and vibrant force in the life of twenty-first century believers, even though we may not have allowed it to develop to its full potential in our own personal lives. The secularists of our time tell us that Christianity and matters of the Spirit are of little or no concern and irrelevant to our modern sophisticated age. In recent decades we have frequently heard the expression, "religionless Christianity," which implies the dissolution of the spiritual aspects of the faith and the accentuation of the practical applications of the faith in personal and social relationships. In sharp contradiction to such a view, however, great numbers of people are searching for a "spiritual experience" and are rebelling against the culture which has tried with reckless abandon to discard the spiritual. Tragically, many are searching for this "spiritual experience" outside the Christian faith.

There are good reasons to know with assurance that the infinite-personal God of the Bible and historic Christianity does exist, that the Christian faith is patently and demonstrably true, and that we can possess a lively spirituality that may have been lacking before and may yet be lacking in our lives. The faith of Jesus Christ is concerned precisely with the practical, everyday real world that we experience and the real life that we persistently encounter. Christianity has rich resources that can be amazingly satisfying to the spiritual longings in our hearts and lives. The Christian faith refuses to die in spite of the many and mighty forces arrayed against it. Its demise has often been predicted, but it has not died and it is not likely to die anytime soon. It will not and cannot die because our humanity has a religious dimension that cannot fully be realized or fulfilled where faith has been denied or neglected. Harvey Cox admitted that, "Man is more essentially religious than many of us have assumed. He thirsts for mystery, meaning, community, and even for some sort of ritual."[2] Man, even twenty-first century man, needs religion for the total fulfillment of his humanity. Because God created man in his own image, man is a worshipping being (Gen. 1:27). Teilhard de Chardin, in modern philosophical parlance, expressed it well, "The more man becomes man, the more will he become prey to a need, a need that is always more explicit, more subtle and more magnificent, the need to adore."[3]

It will be the purpose of this book to breathe some badly needed vitality into our sometimes flagging spiritual lives. Unless our life in the Spirit is intensified and invigorated, we have no real and living hope, only a barren shadow of the reality which Christ promised to his people. With it refreshed, motivated and strengthened, however, we will be able to charge into life at full steam, fulfilling the hopes that before we hardly dared to cherish. Through an open and honest confrontation of ourselves, our beliefs, and the reality and vitality of our faith, it is altogether possible for us to come to the point where Jesus Christ and the Christian faith again are beautiful, personal and living realities in our otherwise mundane lives. It is obvious that many individuals in our generation deeply desire this. It is then with this worthy and enriching goal before us that we begin our quest for spiritual maturity.

---

[2] Quoted from John Macquarrie. *Paths in Spirituality*. New York: Harper & Row, 1972, p. 3.

[3] Teilhard de Chardin. *Le Milieu Divin*. London: Collins, 1960, p. 118.

Discussion Questions

1. Reflect upon your personal conversion experience and ask yourself if you are satisfied with your spiritual life at this moment in time. What changes do you seek? _____

   _____

   _____
   _____

   _____

2. How does your personal faith compare with biblical faith as presented in the Bible study classroom and from the pulpit?_____

   _____

   _____

   _____

3. How does your faith come into play in your everyday practical life in society? _____

   _____

   _____

   _____

I. Becoming a Christian

In the quest for spiritual maturity, it almost goes without saying that the very basic and fundamental beginning place is that of becoming a Christian. At the onset, however, we must recognize that it is impossible to realize genuine spirituality, in the Christian sense of that word, outside a relationship with God through his Son. This, of course, raises the question of how one becomes a Christian. Many futilely attempt to achieve true spirituality by striving to live according to their personal views of morality, or the views of the particular church with which they are presently associated, absent any real personal encounter with Jesus Christ through his word. Such attempts lead only to discouragement and defeat for, outside a personal relationship with Christ, one is open to the assaults and dominion of Satan's unrelenting forces. Our Lord plainly taught, "Apart from me you can do nothing" (John 15:5). In isolation from Jesus Christ, spiritual achievement is practically and virtually impossible. It is extremely difficult for individuals to work out, on their own terms and within themselves, the high ideals of Christian morality. We see such ideals as it were from a distance. We long to achieve them and make them a very real part of our lives, but they always seem to elude us. By contrast, in Christ we are promised, "No temptation has overtaken you that is not common to man. God is faithful, and he will not let you be tempted beyond your strength, but with the temptation will also provide the way of escape, that you may be able to endure it" (1 Cor. 10:13; cf. Rom. 8:28; 2 Pet. 2:9). In Christ we can also say with the apostle Paul, "I can do all things in him who strengthens me" (Phil. 4:13). In other words, the bold and daring claim of traditional Christianity is that Christ can produce from the smoldering wreck of our broken and wounded lives a new creature that flourishes in a new way to which the old natural man can never aspire or hope to attain.

Is this a possibility for us today? Yes! We need only read the pages of the New Testament to realize that this potential exists. Jesus Christ appeared to the people of his generation and many of them, after confrontation with him, rightly sensed that they had been privileged to stand in the very presence of God. Their heretofore bankrupt and counterfeit lives were transformed by his power and presence into what they came to understand to be an authentic existence. It could be said that their indivisible shackles were removed and they were freed to live as they never before dreamed they would. These individuals were radically transformed into new people. Their old state of wretched sinfulness and the twisted, perverted, and spiritually demented outlook, which had wrecked their prospects and made happiness and fulfillment unattainable for them, was first made impotent and then destroyed. They were not merely improved, or reformed, or altered in any way that meant merely an outward change. They were truly and genuinely remade, or as Paul put it: "Therefore, if anyone is in Christ, he is a new creation; the old has passed away, behold, the new has come" (2 Cor. 5:17). This type of life is not merely a footnote in an ancient book. It is possible for us too, and I believe that most of us really do yearn to realize and enjoy such a life as Paul describes.

When one desires to become a Christian, he cannot remain in a passive situation somehow hoping for some sort of nondescript religious experience to manifest itself to him and eventually to motivate him. Nevertheless, many individuals today are doing just this, waiting expectantly for a time when they "feel" the presence of God, or when they "experience" an emotional moment in their spiritual quest. These individuals are looking for a special and discernible experience to assure them of their relationship with God. They are looking for the wrong thing, and they are searching for it in the wrong place. They are not hungering and thirsting for truth and righteousness, "proceeding forth out of the mouth of God" (Matt. 4:4; cf. 5:6). They are hungering and thirsting for life-altering religious experiences. Such experiences may occur in a few individual lives, and those persons may be remarkably and forever changed by them. They may interpret these special, atypical events as a form of divine communication or sign. But they are, by and large, experiences which are enjoyed by only a few, and their legitimacy and reality are at best highly questionable and at worst lamentable because in the mind of the one so changed God's written word has taken a secondary place to a subjective personal experience, and that is not a desirable end result.

How, then, does one become a Christian, a child of God? This question is simple and its answer is just as simple. One becomes a Christian by accepting Jesus Christ as Lord and Savior! The preceding statement is frequently repeated but seldom fully understood. This is not a theological proposition. Neither is it a pious or mystical statement. It means no more than "to believe," which entails believing all of it or none of it. Now, do not misunderstand what we are trying to say. To appreciate fully the meaning of this assertion requires looking more deeply than a mere glance at the surface. To believe means much more than most people think it means. The real significance of the word is to commit oneself, to trust in God, and to obey his revealed will. No matter how complicated and sophisticated our society may become, no matter how educated or simple an individual may be, all arrive at the destination by the same route, insofar as becoming a Christian is concerned. Just as the mightiest and the most diminutive are brought into this world in the same manner, so too, all men come to God in exactly the same way. This is true for all men and for all ages: "I am the way, and the truth, and the life; no one comes to the Father, but by me," says Jesus in John 14:6 (cf. Matt. 11:27; John 1:18; 6:46). The apostle Peter assures us of this same truth: "There is salvation in no one else, for there is no other name under heaven given among men by whom we must be saved" (Acts 4:12).

It is at this point, however, that so many protest the intrinsic narrowness of this approach and, as a result, ultimately fail to come to God through Christ. We all know about the great religions of the world and we are more or less informed of the nature and tremendous variety of their inspiring literature. We have seen some few truly magnificent characters and noble lives that were produced by such religions and intently have read of them in their great literary productions. It goes against our grain; it rubs us wrong; it sounds unfair and very intolerant for us therefore to say that all people of whatever stripe must come to God in the same manner, that is, through Jesus Christ and him alone. But the Christian religion is concerned not with variegated human opinion, but with absolute truth. It is concerned with that which *is*, not with that which *men think ought to be*. It is not merely a matter of what appeals to an individual; it is a matter of what claims that individual. The simple and unarguable truth that two and two makes four may not appeal to everyone, but it does claim to apply equally and universally to everyone. In the same manner, the truth that all men must come to God through Jesus Christ may not appeal to all in this increasingly secular and "politically correct" environment, but it does claim all. It claims all, for it is truth pure and simple.

Why do all men need to come to Christ? What is the moral necessity behind the demand? The divine requirement for all to unite with Christ is due to the fact that in his present condition man is not "all that he should be" and certainly not "all that he could be." This is true because, as Scripture has everywhere testified, "all have sinned and fallen short of the glory of God" (Rom. 3:23). Even those who argue for the perfectibility of the human race will admit that in his present state man is quite imperfect. The Bible teaches that man was made for something different than the kind of life he has actually chosen and achieved for himself. He has not attained the ideal for which God engineered him. In fact, he has not done well at all. He has not even remained in his initial estate as originally created. There is not much of the image and likeness of God about him. Jesus spoke of the universality of sin when he said, "No one is good but God alone" (Mark 10:18b).

From the very beginning of his history in the Garden of Eden, man has been separated from God due to his unfortunate choice of rebellion over obedience and the resultant moral guilt that inevitably comes in its wake: "Your iniquities have made a separation between you and your God, and your sins have hid his face from you" (Isa. 59:2). All goodness has God as its source. Being separated from God infects the life with moral impotence, further weakens a man and opens him up to the additional assaults of sin. Sin is the sort of spiritual disorder and imbalance which results in alienation from God. It is a turning away from God, a neglecting and forgetting of God. It is pushing God away. Basically, sin is a form of idolatry (perhaps the purest form of all!) – an undisguised effort to found one's life upon man and the finite, rather than upon God and the infinite.

C.S. Lewis refers to this degenerate sin of human idolatry of the self as Pride.[1]

Whatever we call it, pride or selfishness or idolatry, it has been the ruin of man since The Fall. This truth is vividly pointed out in the tragic life of Charles Colson, once an advisor to President Nixon who was convicted, along with others, in the Watergate scandal that riveted the news media and rocked the political fortunes of many in the United States in the 1970s. In a conversation with his good friend Tom Phillips, the highly accomplished and very intelligent Colson was confronted with the fact that his problem was primarily pride, the chief sin that alienates man from God. In trying to assist Colson in developing a relationship with God, Tom Phillips told Colson:

"'Chuck, I don't think you will understand what I'm saying about God until you are willing to face yourself honestly and squarely. This is the first step.' Tom reached to the corner table and picked up a small paperback book. I read the title: *Mere Christianity* by C.S. Lewis.

"'I suggest you take this with you and read it while you are on vacation.' Tom started to hand it to me, then paused. 'Let me read you one chapter.'

"I leaned back, still on the defensive, my mind and emotions whirling.

There is one vice of which no man in the world is free; which every one in the world loathes when he sees it in someone else; and of which hardly any people, except Christians, ever imagine that they are guilty themselves. I have heard people admit that they are bad-tempered, or that they cannot keep their heads about girls or drink, or even that they are cowards. I do not think I have ever heard anyone who was not a Christian accuse himself of this vice....There is no fault...which we are more unconscious of in ourselves. And the more we have it ourselves, the more we dislike it in others.

The vice I am talking of is Pride or Self-Conceit....Pride leads to every other vice: it is the complete anti-God state of mind.

"As he read I could feel a flush coming into my face and a curious

---

[1] C.S. Lewis. *Mere Christianity*. New York: The MacMillian Company, 1971, p. 108.

burning sensation that made the night seem even warmer. Lewis's words seemed to pound straight at me.

...it is Pride which has been the chief cause of misery in every nation and every family since the world began. Other vices may sometimes bring people together: you may find good fellowship and jokes and friendliness among drunken people or unchaste people. But Pride always means enmity – it is enmity. And not only enmity between man and man, but enmity to God.

In God you come up against something which is in every respect immeasurably superior to yourself. Unless you know God as that – and, therefore, know yourself as nothing in comparison – you do not know God at all. As long as you are proud you cannot know God. A proud man is always looking down on things and people: and of course, as long as you are looking down, you cannot see something that is above you.

"Suddenly I felt naked and unclean, my bravado defenses gone. I was exposed, unprotected, for Lewis's words were describing me. As he continued, one passage in particular seemed to sum up what had happened to all of us at the White House:

For Pride is spiritual cancer: it eats up the very possibility of love, or contentment, or even common sense.

"Just as a man about to die is supposed to see flash before him, sequence by sequence, the high points of his life, so, as Tom's voice read on that August evening, key events in my life paraded before me as if projected on a screen. Things I hadn't thought about in years – my graduation speech at prep school – being 'good enough' for the Marines – my first marriage, into the 'right' family – sitting on Jaycee's dais while civic leader after civic leader praised me as the outstanding young man of Boston – then to the White House – the clawing and straining for status and position – 'Mr. Colson, the President is calling – Mr. Colson, the President wants to see you right away.'"

* * * * *

"Now, sitting there on the dimly lit porch, my self-centered past was washing over me in waves. It was painful. Agony. Desperately I tried to defend myself. What about my sacrifices for government service, the giving up of a big income, putting my stocks into a blind trust? The truth, I saw in an instant, was that I'd wanted a position in the White House more than I'd wanted money. There was no sacrifice. And the more I talked about my own sacrifices, the more I was really trying to build myself up in the eyes of others. I would eagerly have given up everything I'd ever earned to prove myself at the mountaintop of government. It was pride – Lewis's 'great sin' – that had propelled me through life.

"Tom finished the chapter on pride and shut the book. I mumbled something non-committal to the effect that 'I'll look forward to reading that.' But Lewis's torpedo had hit me amidships. I think Phillips knew it as he stared into my eyes. That one chapter ripped through the protective armor in which I had unknowingly encased myself for forty-two years. Of course, I had not known God. *How could I?* I had been concerned with myself. *I* had done this and that, *I* had achieved, *I* had succeeded and *I* had given God none of the credit, never once thanking Him for any of His gifts to me. I had never thought of anything being 'immeasurably superior' to myself, or if I had in fleeting moments thought about the infinite power of God, I had not related Him to my life. In those brief moments while Tom read, I saw myself as I never had before. And the picture was ugly.

"'How about it, Chuck?' Tom's question jarred me out of my trance. I knew precisely what he meant. Was I ready to make the leap of faith as he had in New York, to 'accept' Christ?"

* * * * *

"Tom then reached for his Bible and read a few of his favorite psalms. The comforting words were like a cold soothing ointment. For the first time in my life, familiar verses I'd heard chanted lifelessly in church came alive. 'Trust in the Lord,' I remember Tom reading, and I wanted to, right that moment I wanted to – if only I knew how, if only I could be sure.

"'Would you like to pray together, Chuck?' Tom asked, closing his Bible and putting it on the table beside him.

"Startled, I emerged from my deep thoughts. 'Sure – I guess I would – Fine.' I'd never prayed with anyone before except when someone said grace before a meal. Tom bowed his head, folded his hands, and leaned forward on the edge of his seat. 'Lord,' he began, 'we pray for Chuck and his family, that You might open his heart and show him the light and the way....'

"As Tom prayed, something began to flow into me – a kind of energy. Then came a wave of emotion which nearly brought tears. I fought them back. It sounded as if Tom were speaking directly and personally to God, almost as if He were sitting beside us. The only prayers I'd ever heard were formal and stereotyped, sprinkled with *Thees* and *Thous*.

"When he finished there was a long silence. I knew he expected me to pray but I didn't know what to say and was too self-conscious to try. We walked to the kitchen together where Gert was still at the big table, reading. I thanked her and Tom for their hospitality."[2]

Colson later came to the deep and heady realization that all men must one day come to: God is a living, holy, and righteous Being, and when men sin, it is a serious offense against and before this living, holy, and righteous Father of us all. Such sins (intentional or unintentional) are not just psychological guilt-feelings, but are real and tragic provocations against God – violations so odious and objectionable that they nailed a pure and sinless Savior to a cross. Sin is a grievous offense against Love. This truth is established very early in the scriptures as the Old Testament reveals that the sins of the world grieved God to his heart: "The Lord saw that the wickedness of men was great in the earth, and that every imagination of the thoughts of his heart was only evil continually....and it grieved him to his heart" (Gen. 6:5-6). How startling these words are in their directness and definiteness. Yet they reveal the heart-felt grief and pity that God feels because of the misery of his creatures as they live in sin.

The fact of the sinfulness of all men before God is the reason that all men must come to God through Jesus Christ, for only Jesus' atoning and redeeming work on the cross could tear down the man-erected sin-barrier between God and man: "For as by one man's disobedience many were made sinners, so by one man's obedience many will be made righteous" (Rom. 5:19; cf. Mark 10:45; Eph. 1:7; Heb. 2:14-15; 1 Pet. 1:18-19). Once man believes and obeys God

---

[2] Charles W. Colson. *Born Again*. Old Tappan, N.J.: Fleming H. Revell Company, 1977, pp. 112-116.

through Christ, he begins to enjoy a sense of peace with God. He is aware of God's bountiful kindness and has a glorious hope for the future. Through Christ, God has definitively defeated the power of the forces of Satan in our lives: "He has delivered us from the dominion of darkness and transferred us to the kingdom of his beloved Son" (Col. 1:13). To be sure, we will be tested, our inner strength will be tried, but we can rest secure in the unfailing love of God for us in Christ. If God thus came to our assistance when we were his enemies and separated from him by our sins (Rom. 5:8), is it not logical to believe that he will save us from every spiritual peril now that we are his children? Through Christ, God has freed us from bondage to self and sin: "For freedom Christ has set us free....only do not use your freedom as an opportunity for the flesh, but through love be servants of one another" (Gal. 5:1, 13). Thus a new life has been opened up to us, an "abundant life" (cf. John 10:10) of authentic freedom, creativity, and love. We have the possibility of becoming a "new creation" (2 Cor. 5: 17). In so doing we will have obtained more than simply deliverance, more than merely freedom, as wonderful as both may seem. We will have become new creatures altogether, partaking in a new kind and quality of life. Not only will we be thoroughly pardoned, but we will also be enabled to make a fresh start, with a new and better nature, different from what we ever were, even at our very best previously. Our task is to live this new and different life in the freedom and with the power that God has granted to us in Christ.

How may we come to enjoy such a wonderful and carefree lifestyle? The answer is relatively simple. It begins with the recognition that it is the redemptive work of Christ on the cross plus *nothing* on our own part that makes such a life possible for us. The writer of the Epistle to the Hebrews states, "Therefore he is able to save completely ("to the uttermost") those who come to God through him, because he always lives to intercede for them" (Heb. 7:25). Repeatedly he says that Jesus "sat down" when he had accomplished his priestly labor (Heb. 1:3; 8:1; 10:12; 12:1), something which no priest in the Temple was ever permitted to do because their work was never finished (Heb. 10:11; Deut. 18:5). It has been frequently and rightly noted that throughout the scriptures a surprising emphasis is placed on the fact that we may have a close and lasting relationship with our Creator because of God's amazing and enduring grace: "For by grace you have been saved through faith; and this is not your own doing, it is the gift of God" (Eph. 2:8; cf. Rom. 3:23-24; 5:20; 1 Cor. 15:9-10). Grace in one sense may be defined as God's free movement into history whereby he approaches us to transform our existence. This action on God's part does not depend on our works or merits, but is totally spontaneous from the divine side (cf. Rom. 5:8). It is God freely inclining himself toward us for our well-being. And when we accept this grace of God by coming to him through Jesus Christ, the scriptures say we stand before our Creator justified, cleansed from sin, and in fellowship with God. This is the way the Lord has desired it to be from the beginning. The apostle Paul puts it in these terms: "You were washed, you were sanctified, you were justified in the name of the Lord Jesus Christ in the Spirit of our God" (1 Cor. 6:11).

God's grace is the instrument of man's redemption, and the instrument man must employ to gain access to that grace is faith. The faith of which we speak is not to be identified with the Kierkegaardian concept of faith as a leap in the dark, nor is it the popular modern concept of "passive trust" or "belief only." A great number of people believe that God exists, yet many of these same individuals live as if he did not. Neither is this salvation faith to be identified with any idea which promotes the robotic performance of a certain number of religious chores or the fulfillment of a long list of "good deeds." Salvation faith is that deep faith that entails a commitment of one's life to a full trust in God and the worthiness of his desires for man. Salvation faith is not a mere intellectual ascent to a religious proposition either, for "even the demons believe – and shudder," says James (Jas. 2:19). James is here speaking against mere propositional belief – acceptance of the proposition that "God is." Salvation faith is belief in Jesus Christ, which implies intellectual and emotional assent to his teachings, coupled with an attitude of trust, loyal obedience, and faithfulness.

From this we recognize that faith is only real when it is accompanied by humble obedience. And obedience is not only the consequence of faith; it is also the presupposition of faith. The two are not chronological. We may like to think that we believe first and obey later, but the truth of the matter is that we cannot believe unless we obey. Faith is not a transient act or a passing emotion, but the commitment of the whole self to Jesus Christ and the splendid truth of his Gospel. There is only one faith and that is one that motivates the heart to humble obedience, and only one obedience, namely that which takes its initiative from trusting faith. Such faith always demands a radical step on the part of the faithful, one symbolized by the apostle Peter leaving his nets, Levi leaving the customs office, Paul abandoning his Pharisaic roots, and so forth. To us, it may only involve a response to the command of the Lord to be "born again" (cf. Acts 2:38; Gal. 3:27), yet even this corollary may be too radical for many. Make no mistake about it, it is necessary, however, for this new birth puts us into Christ and into an abiding relationship with God.

Discussion Questions

1. What do you think about the apostle Paul's claim that he "can do all things in him [Christ] who strengthens" him (Phil. 4:13). Is this true in your life? _____

2. To accept Jesus Christ as Lord and Savior means what in your personal life? _____

   _____

   _____

3. How do you feel about Jesus' statement that all people must come to God through him? Is this a comfortable thing for you to say in today's world? _____

   _____

   _____

4. How do you feel about describing spiritual pride as idolatry? __

   _____

   _____

5. Define salvation faith, or a faith that saves, and how it relates to one's intellect, emotions and obedience. _____

   _____

   _____

II. After the New Birth

Once we have come to God in dependent, trusting, and obedient faith, the Scriptures assure us that we have passed into a new existence. In Christ we die to our old way of life, as symbolized in the act of water baptism, and we are raised to a new life as children of God. We have thus become members of his eternal spiritual kingdom. This new birth is an actual experience made real and accurately pictured through baptism, as vividly set forth by Paul:

> Do you not know that all of us who have been baptized into Christ Jesus were baptized into his death? We were buried therefore with him by baptism into death, so that as Christ was raised from the dead by the glory of the Father, we too might walk in newness of life.

> For if we have been united with him in a death like his, we shall certainly be united with him in a resurrection like his. We know that our old self was crucified with him so that the sinful body might be destroyed, and we might no longer be enslaved to sin. For he who has died is freed from sin (Rom. 6:3-7).

This apostle further assures us that "if any one is in Christ, he is a new creation; the old has passed away, behold, the new has come" (2 Cor. 5:17; cf. John 3:3-8; 1 Pet. 1:3, 23). When one is baptized into Christ, he takes the beginning step in a process that eventually and radically transforms him into a new person. The old state of sinfulness and the past broken, perverted outlook is on its way out. In Christ we are not merely improved, or reformed, or altered in any way which results in a mere external change. We are remade! Our thoughts, ambitions, and lives are no longer centered on self but on Christ and others. And this transformation process is from God: "All this is from God, who through Christ reconciled us to himself" (2 Cor. 5:18). Thus, God's gracious redemptive act in Christ was not only an event that was what it was without regard to human consciousness or response. On the contrary, from the beginning it was conceived as consisting precisely in a decisive reorientation of man's entire conscious, perceptual, emotional and frequently obstinate and willful inner being.

This new birth is where many of us slip and falter, however. It is essential, therefore, that we understand that while the new birth is necessary, it is *only the beginning* of a much more extensive process. We must not think that once we have been baptized into Christ and belong to him, through the agency of this adoptive process, that this is all there is to it. The new birth ought to be an awakening of the human mind to its own opportunities and responsibilities as a new creation before God. It is marked by a definite commitment to the will and purpose of God, and by a clear change of attitude and direction of life. The sad fact, however, is that becoming a Christian with its resultant spiritual awakening and conviction is a reality in far too few lives. Again, we can draw a parallel between the spiritual birth and the physical birth. The fact that we are physically born is important (if it had not happened, we would not be here), but in a sense isn't the physical birth the least important aspect of our life? Billions have been born, lived for a while and then died without making much of a mark on the world. After this birth, this introduction to the physical world, the important thing is that we can begin to live a life worth living and develop our potentials. It is exactly the same thing in relation to our new birth as Christians. Here too, after our initial public act of decision and obedience, the important next step is that we begin living as a recreated child of God. This "living" begins at the new birth, persists throughout our present earthly life, and sees its ultimate fulfillment when our Lord comes again. There should result such a complete transformation of the mind, emotions, and will that it can only be described as it is in the New Testament, a "new birth", a whole-hearted turning to God and away from the old life.

After rising from the watery grave of baptism, having died to our old way of life (cf. Rom. 6:6), we normally ask the question, "What must I do now that I am a Christian?" At this point we are usually directed to a list of things, often negative, to do and not to do. This list usually varies, not entirely of course, but as regard the particular culture and times in which we live, there will be differences. If one accomplishes all the things on the list, he is assured in his mind that he will be spiritual and therefore well-pleasing to God. If nothing more than this, then one will at the very least regard himself as representing a higher and more complete form of the faith than those who do not manifest a solid effort toward living up to all the things found on the list. The fact is that often such self-imposed "paralegal" requirements result in an artificial and perfunctory stringency which goes far beyond anything demanded by our Lord. Reality shows us, however, that we do not necessarily become more spiritual by keeping all the "laws" which might appear on such a list. Even if the list contained some very excellent things, spirituality involves much more than merely refraining from certain external taboos and performing a certain number of good works. This propensity is clearly evident in the lives of the scribes and Pharisees of Jesus' day. The fact is that such lists, in many cases at least, have a tendency to promote an attitude of arrogance and self-righteousness. They provide for a predisposition toward unloving attitudes in regard to others who may not be so disposed. Those who do not live up to these "lists" are often regarded as dangerous heretics, profligate sinners, or somehow less than fully Christian, and occasionally it is judged that relentless war must be waged against them. Thus, such pious legalism becomes a pretentious but counterfeit way of serving God that is on the one hand bogus, but on the other quite congenial to man's pride and thus an easy entrapment for us. We begin to develop an entirely external righteousness and learn to depend altogether on the outward aspects of God's will and purpose and never develop that necessary quality of inner righteousness and soulful spirituality which genuine Christianity demands. The true test of the reality and sincerity of one's religion, however, does not lie solely in the observance of outward regulations, or in one's actions in regard to fulfilling the ceremonial aspects of the law (as understood by the law-keeper). Rather, the real test of the reality and sincerity of one's religion lies in the individual's relationship, attitude, and love toward God and his fellow man. It is what the Christian thinks and desires, coupled with the condition of the heart that determines the genuineness of one's spirituality.

In an effort to combat this very evident tendency toward outward legalism, another group observes the fallacy of this approach and begins to work against this "list of taboos" concept by preaching a splendid funeral oration for all such externalism. This group asks,

"Did not Paul write, 'Christ is the end of the law'?" (Rom. 10:4). Since all are justified by God's free grace and not at all by human merit, there is no logical reason or spiritual obligation to strive to keep track of such lists of dos and don'ts, much less concern ourselves with doing the "dos" and avoiding the "don'ts." That method of trusting in a meticulous observance of certain requirements to attain spirituality is a mistake, according to their way of thinking. Many of these become blind to their own tendency toward "lawlessness" (antinomianism), however, and their general disregard for careful observance of God's will (Matt. 7:21-23). Thus a struggle is created within Christendom between those who seem to stress meticulous obedience to a list of rules and regulations on the one hand, and those who appear to emphasize little or no restrictions at all on the other. Both ways of thinking have right and wrong aspects of their special viewpoints, depending on how and with what emphasis they approach the subject. It is not our purpose in this particular work to explore the several proclivities or logical inconsistencies on the one side or the other of this intriguing but onerous subject; rather, we are about the task of emphasizing that which directs us toward genuine inner spirituality. What we must realize, therefore, is that we do not advance toward true spirituality by carefully keeping a "list," nor do we come to spiritual maturity by rejecting such lists and living a decadent or licentious lifestyle. Neither of these will take us where we would like to go. True spirituality must be something far deeper than either of these concepts.

It is the conviction of this writer that the so-called "orthodox" mentality has been, by and large, of the "list" type. Most individuals within the Christian community have viewed genuine faith as careful and conscientious obedience to a list of "Thou shalts" and "Thou shalt nots." If true spirituality is to be attained, we confirm that this mentality must be set aside, but in so saying we do not imply that our only alternative to it is for us to adopt a libertinistic attitude. In referring to such blatant libertinism, the apostle Paul says, "God forbid" (Rom. 6:2, KJV). There is more than ample emphasis in the New Testament writings against such silly libertinism and just as much emphasis in support of a more legalistic stringent ethical life. Paul recognized that the believer is given the power essential to live an ethical life. His point is not that the Christian *should* not continue in sin, but that he *will* not, and *cannot* continue in sin: "How can we who died to sin still live in it?" (Rom. 6:2). No matter how much we may try to convince ourselves that living the lifestyle of a libertine equates to our being more open and mature, such reasoning is preposterous and morally wrong. In Christ we have died to such world philosophies (Col. 2:8). As a new creation we have been imbued with a new ethical motive and a fresh spiritual power so that we cannot identify with either legalism or libertinism, but only with our Lord and his desire to do the will of the Father not of constraint, but freely and willingly (Matt. 6:10; 7:21; 12:50; 26:39, 42; etc.). We "walk in newness of life" (Rom. 6:4).

When we push out of our minds the small, trite list of rules and regulations that we may have adopted in the past, where do we find ourselves, and what do we then confront head-on and wrestle with in our earnest quest for spiritual maturity? Certainly not Pharisaic legalism or profligate libertinism, but instead we are confronted with soul-gripping and heart-wrenching concepts such as the following, "If your brother is being injured by what you eat, you are no longer walking in love. Do not let what you eat cause the ruin of one for whom Christ died" (Rom. 14:15). Or "You shall love the Lord your God with all your heart, and with all your soul, and with all your mind....You shall love your neighbor as yourself" (Matt. 22:37, 39). Or again, "Go, sell what you possess and give to the poor,... and come, follow me" (Matt. 19:21). Here are some arresting absolute declarations far weightier than any "Thou shalts" or "Thou shalt nots," which we have encountered in our experience with list-making and list-keeping. Others fit in this same category: "Sinning against your brethren and wounding their conscience when it is weak, you sin against Christ. Therefore, if food is a cause of my brother's falling, I will never eat meat, lest I cause my brother to fall" (1 Cor. 8:12-13); once more "This commandment we have from him, that he who loves God should love his brother also" (1 John 4:21).

While we certainly cannot claim for ourselves any personal merit by living according to these fundamental principles, and while we cannot accomplish them by our own strength alone, or perfectly in life, they remain continually before our minds and hearts as demanding divine imperatives and road signs marking the way to authentic spiritual maturity. So when we purge our minds of all superficial "lists," we are then confronted not with the prospect of a looser, more reckless and personally more decadent and wanton lifestyle, but with a much more profound and heart-searching set of demands than any previous list of rules and regulations have encompassed. We are confronted with the hard reality of genuinely and earnestly loving God and others in precisely the manner in which Jesus loved the Father. This demanding love is the infallible goal of a life that wishes to move past legalistic list-keeping and the false freedom of wanton libertinism. This love is the true sign of the reality and fidelity of our faith, the first fruit of the Spirit, and the greatest of all Christian graces. Paul puts it in this manner: "For in Christ Jesus neither circumcision nor uncircumcision is of any avail, but faith working through love....the fruit of the Spirit is love" (Gal. 5:6, 22; cf. 1 Cor. 13:2, 8, 13).

Earlier we quoted Paul as saying that Christ was the "end of the law" (Rom. 10:4; cf. Gal. 2:4), in that our Lord brought freedom from the law's tyranny over the lives of those who have been liberated by his saving work. But again, this liberty from the law is not equal to moral or ethical license; in point of fact it is just the opposite. It is the freedom to love and live victoriously. The Christian life is to be contrasted in the boldest manner possible with the life of self-centered indulgence as well as with the life of legalistic conformity. The Jews in the time of Christ had fallen into a form of pitiful bondage to the Law of Moses, but the declaration of the apostle Paul is that Christian faith includes only free, emancipated people. Sin had its seat of power in the flesh and was awakened and acknowledged by the law's ability to define it as such. Contrariwise, the law may define what is good, but in the end it is powerless to produce it. However hard a sinful man may struggle to make himself conform to the intricate requirements of the law he will always in the end be the same transgressor and law breaker at heart. The law lacked the ability to alter the human heart. Into this situation Jesus interjected himself in order to destroy the power that sin had over the human family and abrogate the law with its multitude of stipulations and regulations. The result is that Christians are freed from this frustration and failure in order to live by the Spirit and no longer by the letter of the law: "If you are led by the Spirit you are not under the law" (Gal. 5:18); "While we were living in the flesh, our sinful passions, aroused by the law, were at work in our members to bear fruit for death. But now we are discharged from the law, dead to that which held us captive, so that we serve not under the old written code but in the new life of the Spirit" (Rom. 7:5-6). Yet, if we persist in the old way of living and allow our lives to be dominated by legalism and tyrannized by rule-keeping, we have reverted to the very thing from which Christ has come to deliver us.

We cannot, however, over-emphasize the fact that such freedom from the law does not mean that we live in spiritual anarchy, or anti-nomianism, that is, as a people devoid of religious directive, without a law. If a sinner hears that God stands ready to forgive all of his sins and thus presumes on this basis to do anything he pleases, regardless of its possible harmful effect on other people or what God's will for him and his life may be, he is then foolishly giving full rein to his sinful nature. Even though, as Paul points out twice in his Corinthian letter (and as the lawless man would echo repeatedly *ad infinitum*), "All things are lawful" (1 Cor. 6:12; 10:23), all things are not wholesome, all things do not build up, nor do they lead inevitably toward spiritual maturity. In fact, some things are downright destructive and debilitating. They will wreck the life and torture the soul. The man of faith is free from such, but he must not again become a slave through his celebration of his newfound liberty. His freedom must not, at the end of the day, force him back into his chains and re-enslave him, rather he must learn to live in his blessed freedom in such a manner as to demonstrate that he has learned from Jesus Christ the great lessons the Lord intended for us all to embrace. And thus, he loves God and his neighbor, seeking their highest good, not his own self-interest. This love is Christ's unique brand of love and on that account it looks past selfish motives and recognizes the joyful burden of personal responsibility. This is the life God meant for us to have, so possessed and motivated by the beneficent love of God in Christ that out of abundant gratitude and reciprocal love it freely seeks to do all that love demands, not haltingly or grudgingly but with joy and gladness.

The Christian life, therefore, is lived between the extremes. It is neither a life of rabid legalism nor of dissipated libertinism, but one characterized by inward spiritual reality and appropriate response to God's will for us. This principle has always been applicable to the human situation. It was even true under the Law of Moses, as is so clearly seen in the Ten Commandments: "You shall not covet..." (Ex.

20:17). Here, in the midst of the setting forth of requisite legislation in the Mosaic Law, is the reality of the fact that the inner life ultimately determines destiny. All good and evil thoughts and acts originate in the heart, as so emphatically taught: "Hear and understand: not what goes into the mouth defiles a man, but what comes out of the mouth, this defiles a man....what comes out of the mouth proceeds from the heart, and this defiles a man. For out of the heart come evil thoughts, murder, adultery, fornication, theft, false witness, slander" (Matt. 15:10-11, 18-19). Acting in a certain way tells us nothing about the thinking of the person whose actions we observe. Simple observation of the action does not reveal what is going on in the mind. Likewise, an external act of righteousness does not assure one of spirituality because it does not inform us regarding the motivation behind the righteous act. If this were possible, the scribes and Pharisees of Jesus' day would have been standing at the pinnacle of spirituality, and the Lord would have complimented them accordingly. Their outward obedience to the law and incessant professions of piety motivated everyone to think of them as paragons of virtue. No one could hope to be as good as they were in relation to outward sanctity and genuine holiness, yet Jesus said of them, "Unless your righteousness exceeds that of the scribes and Pharisees, you will never enter the kingdom of heaven" (Matt. 5:20). Their religion was external in the extreme. It so concentrated on exteriority that inward spirituality was almost entirely neglected. In the end their obsession with the outward dimensions of the law inhibited their spiritual growth and stunted their personal piety.

Interestingly, it was the Mosaic commandment, "You shall not covet," that made the apostle Paul so keenly aware of his own personal sinfulness:

> What then shall we say? That the law is sin? By no means! Yet, if it had not been for the law, I should not have known sin. I should not have known what it is to covet if the law had not said, "You shall not covet." But sin, finding opportunity in the commandment, wrought in me all kinds of covetousness. Apart from the law sin lies dead. I was once alive apart from the law, but when the commandment came, sin revived and I died; the very commandment which promised life proved to be death to me. For sin, finding opportunity in the commandment, deceived me and by it killed me. So the law is holy, and the commandment is holy and just and good (Rom. 7:7-12).

Deep dismay swept over the apostle as he came to the realization that God demanded not just the outward act, but the inward desire to do right and act right. Paul did not mean to imply that he was perfect when he said, "I should not have known sin" or "I should not have known what it is to covet." What he intended to communicate was that he did not realize that he was a sinner, at least not in the fullest sense attainable. Why? Because he perceived himself as keeping all of the external laws he was aware of. He had been measuring up to all of the various external forms of the Jewish religion. But now he was awakened to the hideous reality that he was a common sinner who stood justly condemned due to twisted and distorted inward desires: "the very commandment which promised life proved to be death for me" (vs. 10). He understood that he could not alone measure himself against the externalized form of his accustomed rule-keeping but must also measure himself honestly in terms of his inward desire. When we move beyond our pitiful attempts at advancing in spirituality by methodically, mechanically, outwardly, and legalistically trying to keep the commandments, and appraising ourselves as "righteous" on this flawed and defective basis without any concern for the inward motivation of our heart, then we are on the way toward authentic maturity in Christ. Clearly this is one of those important steps which develops us into truly spiritual men and women of God, children of our heavenly Father and dedicated disciples of Jesus the Master Teacher.

Discussion Questions

1. The biblical design for baptism details what in relation to mode and spiritual results?_____

   _____

2. What are the strengths and weaknesses of following one's baptism with a commitment to a list of biblical demands to do and not to do? _____

   _____

   _____

3. Explain the apostle Paul's statement that "Christ is the end of the law" (Rom. 10:4) in relation to legalism on the one hand and lawlessness on the other. _____

_____

_____

_____

4. Does the Old Testament place any emphasis on the value of
    one's inner spirituality over against its emphasis on keeping the
    commandments? Explain. _____

_____

_____

III. Loving God

As we grow in our realization of the supremacy of heart-commitment over rule-commitment in reference to our relationship with God, we are eventually confronted with the challenging words of our Lord: "You shall love the Lord your God with all your heart, and with all your soul, and with all your mind....and....You shall love your neighbor as yourself" (Matt. 22:37, 39). Love for God and for one's neighbor involves internal factors that automatically produce altogether wholesome external manifestations. These represent nothing more than the natural outgrowth of a deep-seated commitment to that which is righteous and good (cf. 1 John 3:16-18). When we do not possess this internal love or commitment, we cannot properly accomplish the concomitant fruit-bearing or demonstrative external works that grow naturally and effortlessly out of this loyalty. So, inwardly we tend to remain sterile, empty and shallow, lacking in any real spirituality.

It is imperative therefore that we recognize that in God's sight the inward is the most important aspect, the area where the greatest emphasis must be placed. Therefore, when we are confronted with the demands which God places upon us in the form of his commands, we must learn to respond to them first of all from within. This is the way which unerringly leads us toward that perfect freedom in Christ about which we speak so longingly. Under this pleasant rubric, we strive fully to accomplish the will of God because that will is first impressed upon us from within. And this same demand upon us from within encompasses a promise from God that he will help us patiently and faithfully to meet such requirements as love may impose. This faithful love, or internal spiritual commitment (however you may choose to describe it), both demands something from us and gives something to us. It places inward claims upon us, of course, but it also provides us with the necessary power so that we might be able to fulfill all of its salutary demands. Vacuous and heartless law-keeping, on the other hand, demands that we respond outwardly by fulfilling specific requirements, yet offers us no power at all to aid us in achieving the goal toward which we strive. At the end of the day it is a road leading nowhere.

The vacant outward obedience that was accompanied by no real inward desire to please God bereft of real spirituality was one of the things that prompted one of Jesus' most negative accusations against the scribes and Pharisees of his generation: "Woe to you, scribes and Pharisees, hypocrites! For you...are full of extortion and rapacity....for you are like white-washed tombs, which outwardly appear beautiful, but within...are full of dead men's bones and all uncleanness" (Matt. 23:25, 27). The concern of these hollow religious leaders to satisfy *only* the external aspect of the law, while neglecting the profounder aspects of true religion, made them the unconscious carriers of a fatal infection. The common people, unable to look below the surface of the impressive outward piety of these religious leaders, often were victims of the identical contagion. And, as a result of the pompous but convincing attitudes of the antagonistic scribes and Pharisees, the people were unaware that these petty men were profoundly wrong and inwardly defiled and carriers of a deadly spiritual poison. Men were deceived by their stalwart and imminently correct outward deportment and so put their trust in them, only to be defiled and corrupted themselves by their exceedingly subtle but distressing virulent infection. What God desires to see in the lives of his people, by contrast, is not correct outward deportment alone, but what he only can give – the inward desire for right living which is kindled and fostered by the love of God and by the comfort and advocacy of his Holy Spirit within.

This internal necessity of selfless love, or commitment to God and neighbor, is what reveals to us our deep need for a Savior. As a subtle and unconscious ploy, we may at times be tempted to compare ourselves against ourselves, as did those proud, self-satisfied Christian brethren at Corinth (cf. 2 Cor. 10:12, 18), and note with some amount of twisted satisfaction that we are better off than many others seem to be at this business of rule-keeping. In fact, such comparisons might for a time tend to make us feel that we are getting along quite well. But when we actually come to grips with God's demand for inward love and loyal commitment (Matt. 5:48), then we are brought down to hard reality by the realization of our true circumstances. We are reminded of the publican who prayed alone for mercy and forgiveness in the temple (Luke 18:13) or of a beleaguered King David, who out of a heart filled with sadness and grief, said, "Have mercy on me, O God, according to thy steadfast love....Create in me a clean heart, O God, and put a new and right spirit within me" (Psa. 51:1, 10). The first and most important preliminary and preparatory thing which Christ does for us as truly receptive believers is to show us that we are not as good as we think we are. This is not a lesson that we want to hear, but it is one we assuredly need: "No one is good but God alone" (Mark 10:18). We cannot rightfully boast of any work that we have ever done, or even claim the privilege of any credit to our own account. And, if we are seeking and hoping to find peace in the thought that we are at least as good as our neighbor, we have never realized the true glory and unique holiness of Christ. When John was given a vision of the Lord, his reaction was altogether predictable: "When I saw him, I fell at his feet as though dead. But he laid his right hand on me, saying, "Fear not, I am the first and the last, and the living one. I died, and behold I am alive forevermore, and I have the keys of Death and Hades" (Rev. 1:17-18).Thus, any attempt, as it were, to stand spiritually erect before God due to our ability to keep the things we have on our particular "list" is futile.

From reflection upon this heaven-centered emphasis we recognize that the Christian ideal is a standard of divine judgment so far above our own petty conceits and faulty human guidelines that it continually condemns and purifies our personal ideals. We may keep with great diligence all of the outward rituals and observe carefully all of the regulations commanded by our Lord. We may worship faithfully, sing with enthusiasm, give sacrificially, commune regularly, and do all the other outward things "required" of Christians. We may perform all these things with absolute regularity and be a conspicuous public presence at all of the right religious occasions, however, and still be missing something. We may not, even in the face of all this, have our heart, soul, and mind committed to God. Therefore, we cannot pride ourselves in our ability to keep what we have put on our own special "list." We can only answer our Lord and God in a fashion similar to that of the patriarch Job after he had been suitably humbled: "I have uttered what I did not understand, things too wonderful for me, which I did not know....therefore I despise myself, and repent in dust and ashes" (Job 42:3, 6).

This newfound concern in the direction of an internal love for and inward commitment to God simultaneously leads us toward a de-emphasis on the outward show of religion, and this at first may stun us. On this account we may well come to understand in short order why others have chosen to take the other route. We may ask ourselves: Isn't it so much easier to attend to the outward and ritualistic aspects of the Christian faith than those matters inward? By attending to the outward we can much more comfortably latch on to those concrete things that we can point to as our personal accomplishments and, as a result, feel fairly good about our selves. When we place our trust in these external acts, we may tend to feel secure and reassured because effortlessly and thoughtlessly we can keep a number of them, and perhaps even all of them. This, in turn, makes us feel that God is with us due to our ability to do these things. Yet deep down inside we realize that it is personally unsatisfying and ultimately unrewarding to live such a lifestyle characterized only by outward religion devoid of inward reality. It is not that the outward form and ritual are wrong in and of themselves, for if they are commanded by God that could never be true; rather it is that religion is deeper and more profound than just this. The external observances are a very important part of a godly person's life, in fact he may not survive spiritually without them, but there must also be an inward righteousness, and he certainly will not survive spiritually with it. Religion is not just one aspect of life, but is the whole of life. It is not just what we do; it is who we are and what we are.

So this awkward and perhaps unpleasant realization places us in a fretful dilemma. The outward obedience to external ritual is much easier and less demanding in every instance, but deep down within the soul, the sincere Christian will long for something more than this frequently thoughtless regimen of religious activities. We long for a total inner commitment to our God and a genuine sense of his presence and power in our lives. How do we motivate ourselves to love the Lord God with all of our heart, soul, mind, and strength, and our neighbor in the way that we do ourselves? This question is so very important in our quest for spiritual maturity, for Jesus said, "On these two commandments depend all the law and the prophets"

(Matt. 22:40). The Lord has made it clear that the epicenter of the Christian faith is maturing spiritually to a point where we are able to love God and neighbor. Without these two important principles at the heart of our devotions, all external acts of worship in the world will prove meaningless and feel vacuous. As Amos the prophet so vividly expressed this concept as it pertained to the meaningless rituals of his contemporaries in North Israel, external acts without inward piety are such that God "hate[d]...despise[d]...[took] no delight in.... [would] not accept...[would] not look upon....[wanted to] take away... [would] not listen [to]" (Amos 5:21-23) such empty religious words and activities. These are strong terms indeed and they should move us to examine closely and contemplate fully the quality and depth of our own personal religion.

Let us pose the question once more: How do we motivate ourselves to love God with all our heart, soul, mind, and strength? Many Christians lose their way along the path toward spiritual growth because they do not manifest genuine and persistent gratitude toward God. The fact is that the apostle Paul in various contexts associates the most serious spiritual and moral failures with an ungrateful spirit (cf. Rom. 1:21-25). A heart that feels genuine gratitude will manifest its thankfulness in a variety of ways; an ungrateful spirit will show itself in certain ways also. So, giving thanks to God is a very real test for the depth and genuineness of our love. Paul writes, "But fornication and all impurity or covetousness must not even be named among you, as is fitting among saints. Let there be no filthiness, nor silly talk, nor levity, which are not fitting; but instead let there be thanksgiving" (Eph. 5:3-4). In this list of prevalent worldly vices, thanksgiving is suggested as that quality which should give proper tone to the Christian's relationship with God. The very spirit of Christianity must be a spirit of humble gratitude – gratitude for who God is, for what he has shown his people about himself, and for what he has done so selflessly and sacrificially on our behalf. We must therefore continually remind ourselves of the goodness of God which has been so generously lavished upon us, lest in our busyness and carelessness we forget the full magnitude of his many blessings. Such awareness has the potential to be an impenetrable barrier of all God-denying vices and the open gateway to loving God as we should.

This idea of thankfulness is even more emphatically set forth in

Ephesians 5:20 where the apostle Paul admonishes Christians to live in such a manner that they are "always and for everything giving thanks in the name of our Lord Jesus Christ to God the Father." The importance of this is seen in the story of the ten lepers healed by Jesus' compassion and power (Luke 17:11-19). Of the ten, only one returned to give thanks to Christ. In similar fashion, those of us who make our way back to God with grateful hearts will be among the individuals who make up his kingdom. Those of us who fail to demonstrate genuine gratitude will also fail to inherit the kingdom. Why is this so? This will be the case because the dominating attitude of one's life will be determined by the presence or absence of a spirit of thanksgiving. There is something special and enduring about a faith that gives thanks. If we are not grateful toward God, our relationship with him and awareness of him becomes blurred by those factors which dominate our existence, just as it was blurred in the life of the nine lepers who, in their joy at being healed of the horrible disease of leprosy failed to give thought to the one who had made it all possible, and so did not return to give thanks. Only when we take the time and make the effort to manifest that quality of life - gratitude toward God - can we in our own spiritual brokenness be made spiritually whole.

Notice that in Ephesians 5:20 Paul urges us to be giving thanks for *everything*. This *everything*, or "all things" (KJV), is mentioned also in Romans: "We know that in *everything* God works for good" (Rom. 8:28). Everything is just that, everything! We are not to give thanks in all things *except* sorrow or all things *except* tribulation, but are to give thanks in *all* things! Unless thanksgiving can understand unfortunate circumstances as the blessings that they are intended to be, and withstand life's cruel blows and painful denials, it proves itself to be frivolous and transient. Paul manifested his own possession of this thankfulness in all things and even while imprisoned he could joyfully and thankfully write, "Have no anxiety about anything, but in everything by prayer and supplication with thanksgiving let your requests be made known to God" (Phil. 4:6). Even in the midst of trying times we are to be continuously thanking God. Paul and Silas did this although they had been mercilessly beaten, left bruised and bloody, and lay helpless in stocks inside the Philippian prison (cf. Acts 16:16-34). How was Paul able to do this? What gave him the ability to remain thankful and un-embittered in the midst of such painful persecution? Undoubtedly it was his general outlook concerning all such things, and especially his recognition of the fact that God could even use calamity to advance his cause in the world. The apostle said, "I will all the more gladly boast of my weaknesses, that the power of Christ may rest upon me. For the sake of Christ, then, I am content with weaknesses, insults, hardships, persecutions, and calamities; for when I am weak, then I am strong" (2 Cor. 12:9-10).

From Paul's emphasis in this passage we come to realize that we must pray and be thankful whether in ease or pain, both in prosperity and adversity. Yet we are realistic about such circumstances. We understand that there is a difference between giving thanks *for* something and giving thanks *in* something. It may be impossible to be grateful *for* an overpowering and hurtful experience like a personal tragedy but not impossible to be grateful *in* the very midst of that unfortunate experience. This is the crucial test of the thankful approach to life and Paul passed this test with flying colors during the worst of his many terrible misfortunes. The gratitude which he continuously displayed was always demonstrably portrayed in his own words, with one thing firmly and centrally in mind – to deepen his commitment and love to the Lord. The more grateful he showed himself to be, the more eager he became to consider his whole life as a spiritual experience and a divine obligation, and the same will be true of us. We should try with all of the force of our being to manifest thankfulness to God in every conceivable situation, for we know that he shares even the heaviest of our burdens, is lovingly concerned for our ultimate well being, and is always acting on our behalf and in our best interest long term.

Another passage relating to the importance of thanksgiving in our lives is Colossians 2:6-7, "As therefore you received Christ Jesus the Lord, so live in him, rooted and built up in him and established in the faith, just as you were taught, abounding in thanksgiving." Notice in particular that the apostle informs us that to walk in Christ entails being rooted and built up in him, it also involves being established in the faith, and that it encompasses the notion that we be continuously and forever abounding in thanksgiving. The unfailing mark of a healthy spiritual life and the culminating expression of the Christian's whole life before God is thanksgiving (cf. Col. 1:3, 12; 3:15, 17; 4:2). The selfish enjoyment of God's good gifts without wholehearted demonstration of true thankfulness cannot possibly glorify the Lord or benefit us. Lack of reciprocal love and loyal commitment to God can be a persistence temptation only to those who are not sufficiently grateful to God for his many good gifts. In contrast, a conscious recognition of God's generous bounty consecrates both the gifts and the enjoyment of them to the Lord's service and providence.

A final passage[1] we will notice that deals with thanksgiving is found in Paul's letter to the Thessalonians. It says: "Give thanks in all circumstances; for this is the will of God in Christ Jesus for you" (1 Thess. 5:18). A heart filled to the full with earnest gratitude is one of the important goals of Christian maturity toward which we ought to be striving. We have to learn to practice the difficult art of cultivation not only of faith, but of a grateful faith moment by moment. Over time and with patience our prayer should be, therefore, that which was penned by the brilliant author William Shakespeare, who besought the Lord thus: "O Lord, that lends me life, lend me a heart replete with thankfulness."[2]

We have seen how important thankfulness is in the life of every dedicated Christian. The outward show of religion without a thankful heart can never lead us to develop authentic inner righteousness. Clearly this gratitude is what God desires in our lives. William Law, a well-known minister and writer of 18th century England, set forth this truth magnificently when he wrote,

> For it is certain that whatever seeming calamity happens to you, if you thank and praise God for it, you turn it into a blessing. The true saint is not he who prays most, or fasts most…, who gives most alms or is most imminent for temperance…or justice; but it is he who is always thankful to God, who wills everything that God wills, who receives everything as an instance of God's goodness, and has a heart always ready to praise God for it.

Why is it so exceedingly important for us to be thankful? A close reading Romans 1:18-23 will reveal the apostle's answer to this question:

---

[1] There are several more passages relating to thanksgiving, and they all reveal that this trait is essential to the godly life: Rom. 12:12; Eph. 6:18; Psa. 92:1; 100:4; 107:1; etc.

[2] *Henry VI,* Part II, Act I, sc. 1.20.

"For the wrath of God is revealed from heaven against all ungodliness and wickedness of men who by their wickedness suppress the truth. For what can be known about God is plain to them, because God has shown it to them. Ever since the creation of the world his invisible nature, namely, his eternal power and deity, has been clearly perceived in the things that have been made. So they are without excuse; for although they knew God they did not honor him as God or *give thanks* to him, but they became futile in their thinking and their senseless minds were darkened. Claiming to be wise, they became fools, and exchanged the glory of the immortal God for images resembling mortal man or birds or animals or reptiles."

The central point in evidence here is that the primary sin of these ungodly people described in the passage was simply that they were not thankful (vs. 21). Now by this we do not mean to suggest that this is all the wrong they did, for it is obvious that their wickedness extended into all sorts of other things. But according to this text the beginning of man's rebellion against God is wholly wrapped up in his failure to demonstrate an attitude of thankfulness toward his Maker. As we have already pointed out, sin is basically idolatry, or Pride wearing a thin disguise (as per C.S. Lewis). Pride overpowers and overwhelms thankfulness, for the proud individual gets what he thinks he truly deserves. Take for example, the rich farmer of Luke 12:16-21. He did not give thanks to the One who had enriched him but instead thought that all his goods were for his consumption alone and that they had come to him as the result of his efforts and labor without any help from God. The inexcusableness of such an ungodly attitude is evident in that, being in possession of even a limited knowledge of God, he did not show him the thankfulness which such knowledge ought necessarily and naturally to produce. The fact is that herein is manifested the irascible and petulant idolatry – the refusal to be thankful toward the known Giver of all things. In the words of Paul, "they are without excuse." This leads us to conclude that if we are not faithfully giving thanks to God out of a heart filled with gratitude, we are failing in our obligation to love God as we should. Regardless of our ability to keep up with the external observances of the Christian faith, absent a thankful attitude in our hearts toward God, the outward show will accrue no benefit to the one who dutifully performs them, but will eventually produce death to him who shuts God out of the larger equation.

There is, however, a second aspect that we ought not to forget in our quest for a deeper internal love and more genuine commitment to God. It is encapsulated in the following simple but profound words, "You shall love your neighbor as yourself" (Matt. 22:39). We must all admit that this is an area, even for mature Christians, which we could improve on. Lack of love for our neighbor manifests itself in all sorts of bad behaviors. It is found in envy, covetousness, hatred, and lack of concern, to name but a few. If I envy the abilities of someone else, or covet his goods, I soon find that I dislike that individual, perhaps even hate him. It is important, therefore, that I acknowledge that often I dislike an individual because I am cherishing an improper desire for something that belongs to him. In fact, I might even be happy if he were to lose the object of my desire. It is hard to admit, but this is but a step away from openly causing that individual to experience the loss, either by lying about him, stealing from him, or whatever else we might do toward that regrettable end. This is so well illustrated in David's illicit desire to possess Uriah's wife, Bathsheba (2 Samuel 11). This previously righteous and good man abandoned all of his high principles and stooped to the level of adultery, conspired against her rightful husband, attempted to get him drunk and then tried to deceive him into thinking he was responsible for her pregnancy. When all else failed, at the last he took her for his own through treachery and murder. Moreover, he brought others into his evil plan and thus made them partners in his evil. What this so perfectly illustrates is lack of love, and it is the very thing that John had in mind when he wrote, "Any one who hates his brother is a murderer" (1 John 3:15).

The Christian life is a life that is involved with other people. We are part of a larger group which composes the body of Christ. God intended it that way on purpose. Therefore, as we live in the world we will develop relationships. It is imperative that in such relationships we possess and give clear evidence of the virtues that we hold dear, virtues such as those that are outlined by Paul in his Colossian epistle:

> Put on then, as God's chosen ones, holy and beloved, compassion, kindness, lowliness, meekness, and patience, forbearing one another and, if one has a complaint against another, forgiving each other; as the Lord has forgiven you, so you also must forgive. (Col. 3:12-13)

As God has loved us in Christ and set forth the perfect and eternal standard, so we must grow to a state of maturity where it is possible for us to love our neighbors as ourselves.

In our reflection on the subject of loving our sometimes very unlovable neighbor, the words of the apostle Paul in the chapter on love ring out with timeless relevancy:

> If I speak in the tongues of men and angels, but have not love, I am a noisy gong or a clanging cymbal. And if I have prophetic powers, and understand all mysteries and all knowledge, and if I have all faith, so as to remove mountains, but have not love, I am nothing. If I give away all I have, and if I deliver my body to be burned, but have not love, I gain nothing (1 Cor. 13:1-3).

We know from our previous study that it is impossible to love God without obeying him, and that if one truly loves God, he will be led to give all that he has and is to God. Unless and until this fact is clearly perceived and accepted, one will not obey the gospel joyously, nor will he work freely and unceasingly in the Lord's church. But he that would grow spiritually and inherit life eternal must not stop at loving God. Every other human being is made in the image of deity, according to Scripture. So, the necessary concomitant of this is that he must love his neighbor as himself. This is what Jesus taught, and this is the reasoning behind his emphasis upon it.

The late Dr. J. Ridgly Stroop, of Lipscomb University in Nashville, Tennessee, often commented on the nature of this love this love in his classes:

> Any teaching among us of which this is not the very core, which is not pervaded by this attitude and which is not in complete fulfillment of such a life is certainly defective and if taught in the name of Christ is a distortion, being a misrepresentation of the truth.

And the apostle Paul goes on to state explicitly what such love will be like in our lives.

> Love is patient and kind; love is not jealous or boastful; it is not arrogant or rude. Love does not insist on its own way; it is not irritable or resentful; it does not rejoice at wrong, but rejoices in the right. Love bears all things, believes all things, hopes all things, endures all things (1 Cor. 13:4-7).

The truth of the matter is, however, that many times there is a wide breach between Paul's definition of love and what we observe, even in our own lives. It seems as if we don't know how to love one another. Not understanding God's love, we love like the world around us, which says, "You love me first, then I will love you. But my love will stop if you do not do what I say or as I like."

Once more, we need to be reminded that as Christians, we have been born again. We have God's Spirit abiding within, and the essential first fruit of that Spirit is love. God's very nature is love and he imparts this quality to those willing spiritual partners in whom his Spirit dwells. This love is of the type and nature that draws us to others, regardless of their background, social position, lifestyle, or race. Such love and concern for neighbor is not to be understood as a form of philosophical sentimentality, either. It is not even fundamentally emotional. Rather it has, as its very essence and foundation, a heart of unselfishness. It is manifested in its desire to serve, help, and enrich the lives and fortunes of others. Its goal is seeking the highest good for others. Someone has said it well: "Love is that deliberate and fixed attitude of the whole being which puts the best interest of the one we love above our own no matter at what cost to ourselves."

Addressing this important truth as he saw its implications for his own unique situation, Paul unselfishly made the application to himself, and thus teaches us that we must seek the other man's good and not just our own: "'All things are lawful,' but not all things are helpful. 'All things are lawful,' but not all things build up. Let no one seek his own good, but the good of his neighbor" (1 Cor. 10:23-24). In Romans 13:8 Paul says, "Owe no one anything, except to love one another; for he who loves his neighbor has fulfilled the law." In this one respect the Christian is always a debtor, not because of what one person has done for another, but due to what God has done in granting the believer a new life in Christ. Again, we see here the importance of thankfulness. We love our neighbor in conscious gratitude for God's love for us.

> A new commandment I give to you, that you love one another; even as I have loved you, that you also love one another....This is my commandment, that you love one another as I have loved you....This I command you, to love one another (John 13:34; 15:12, 17).

The world in which we live is so impoverished because so many of us who wear the name "Christian" show so little evidence of love for our fellow man. The healing power of the love of God is desperately needed in this world where Satan tempts us to the very opposite. Faith abides because it is a reaction of man to God's offer of salvation. Hope is the result of such faith in the saving and keeping power of Jesus Christ. But it is love that demonstrates the genuineness of that faith and hope.

When we consider the importance of love toward God and love toward our neighbor – this love is the first and the last word about the meaning of the new life in Christ – we will be on our knees as we acknowledge before the Lord Jesus our failure in this area of concern. Such an awareness of our failure will destroy any idea we possess of fulfilling a "list-type" righteousness. It will destroy any tendency toward libertinism, as well as any other superficial view we might have of the Christian lifestyle. Love for God and neighbor is not basically external, but internal, even though it will necessarily make certain outward demands on us. This divine directive, however, reaches down into the very depths of our heart and alters the direction and destiny of the eternal soul. It is in regard to our inward struggle with faith and its everyday application that our problems begin, and so it is in the inner man that our focus on true spirituality becomes blurred and out of focus. The outward sins which inevitably start to multiply in these perfect environmental circumstances are merely the result of inward deterioration. And by the same token, if we are to succeed in our challenging quest for spiritual maturity, we must start first from within. Simply stated, we must learn to love God with all our heart, soul, mind, and strength, and our neighbor as ourself.

Discussion Questions

1. How were the people of Jesus' day defiled and corrupted spiritually by their religious leaders? Is this possible today? _____

    _____

    _____

    Comment. Religion is not just one aspect of life, but is the whole life.

2. How does gratitude to God relate to my spiritual growth? _____

    _____

_____

_____

3. How does our relationship with our others relate to our spiritual
    growth and development? _____

    _____

    _____

    _____

IV. Dying to Self

Up to this point in our study we have discussed what commitment to, or love for God entails. As clearly revealed in the Bible, it involves something much richer and grander than a mere legalistic list-keeping obedience. Too, actual biblical commitment represents a state of affairs that is much more profoundly noble than freewheeling libertinism, an attitude like that which was apparently manifested by some of the less committed Roman Christians (cf. Rom. 6:1). Steadfast loyalty to God, or love for God involves a dying to self, a sacrificing of one's personal wishes and desires. Yes, under the most extenuating circumstances it even involves the willingness to give up one's own life. Our Lord said, "If any man would come after me, let him deny himself and take up his cross and follow me" (Matt. 16:24). If we had lived in Palestine in those days and seen a man carrying his cross, we would have immediately recognized him as a condemned prisoner about to pay the supreme penalty for some wrong done or crime committed. To take up the cross in our own terms today means to put ourselves in the position of a condemned man on the way to his execution.[1] The willingness to lay down one's life is the concrete expression of discipleship. While most Christians will probably not be called upon to literally die a violent death, every Christian must be *willing*, if called upon, to meet this heady condition of discipleship. Herein we see the reality of Christian love for God put to the ultimate test, a love which is far more demanding

---

[1] This self-denial must not be understood as a form of self-contempt, or self-mortification. The fact that we have been forgiven and justified "in Christ" indicates that we have tremendous worth in God's sight. This fact ought to lead us to self-acceptance and self-respect. This is not the same as self-assertion, however, for this would essentially constitute self-centeredness or pride.

than either legalistic list-keeping or self-serving libertinism as the motivating attitude of a consecrated life. In dying to self, we discover one of the most essential building-blocks in our quest toward authentic spiritual maturity reality – dying to self!

There are basically four statements in the New Testament which emphasize the need for the Christian to die to self. Interestingly, they are all found in Romans and Galatians, the general context being Paul's emphasis on grace and faith which surpass the works of the Law of Moses. These we shall summarize as follows:

- "We were buried therefore with him by baptism into death" (Rom. 6:4).

- "We know that our old self was crucified with him" (Rom. 6:6).

- "I have been crucified with Christ; it is no longer I who live" (Gal. 2:20).

- "Far be it from me to glory except in the cross of our Lord Jesus Christ, by which the world has been crucified to me, and I to the world" (Gal. 6:14).

From these scriptures it becomes apparent that the life of a Christian is not summarily a life devoted to keeping a list of rules and regulations of our own devising. Neither is it individual autonomy and emancipation from divine demands. Nor is it a life of rigidly and tirelessly saying "No!" to a series of propositions. Rather, the life of a Christian is fundamentally and regularly saying "No!" to self. As Christians, we are expected to die to self, and not just once at the point of water baptism, but *daily*[2] and therefore persistently in the individual life. This is where the rubber really meets the road. Every day we are to renew the terms of our unconditional surrender to Jesus Christ by constantly denying self and unwaveringly dying to self. Surrounded by a world that almost refuses to say "No!" to anything, and most particularly and especially to self, we as dedicated disciples of Jesus are exhorted to say "No!" firmly and frequently to self.

To deny self means to surrender to the Lord God the usual and customary rights which we have in the past controlled and held do-

---

[2] Luke's version of Matthew 16:24 adds the word "daily" to Christ's demand for taking up the cross (cf. Luke 9:23).

minion over with respect to our own lives. And this self-denial is not just giving up things. That would be easy. It is not to deny things to oneself, but rather to deny control over the self to oneself. It is to say "No!" to self and "Yes!" to the Lord, to repudiate utterly and absolutely the God-denying aspect of the self and wholly acknowledge the Lordship of Jesus Christ in our lives.

Now, admittedly, we cannot think of this aspect of discipleship very long without feeling uncomfortable. But in order to understand it we must face it head on. In reality, looking at it with brutal honesty, are not most of the commands of Jesus that we find difficult those very commands which go up against our own intimate preferences and leave us smarting on the inside because it is not the way we would have handled the situation on our own? Aren't most of our thorniest spiritual problems due to the fact that we have a hard time saying "No!" to self? Somehow, in the midst of all of this inner turmoil and personal struggle, we must train ourselves to acknowledge that our Lord does not ask of us anything that is not for our highest good. His cause is always noble, and his purposes for us are ever in our own and his best interest. This realization, coupled with his promise that when our desires conflict with his will, he will empower us to do his will if we will but lean upon his strength, ought to move us continually forward in our quest for spiritual maturity.

We live in a culture and in a time, however, that does not take kindly to the idea of saying "No!" to self. And try as we may, this attitude fits very easily and comfortably into our own natural disposition also, for we are not generally or characteristically disposed to the practice of saying "No!" to ourselves. We want very intensely to be at the center of our own lives. That almost goes without saying! It is difficult to abandon the deeply rooted attachments of this present world and accustom ourselves to this self-denying lifestyle which Jesus of Nazareth imposes upon us. The lifestyle of Jesus calls upon us to die to the self and enter into a new kind of existence which is fraught with the risks of suffering, rejection, and even death. So, intellectually we have a tendency to rebel against the very thought of this perilous appeal which induces us to die to self.

This rebellion against the notion of dying to self is not something new, however. The fact is that it has been on the scene since the very beginning of the existence of man. This attitude of selfishness and rebellion was the very cause of the Fall. Man wanted to be like God. He did not want to say "No!" to self, even though God commanded him in no uncertain terms to say "No!" So when Satan tempted man, he of course lied to him but he also lured him in with a false promise, "You will not die...you will be like God" (Gen. 3:4-5). Man made the fateful decision to put himself first, at the center of his existence. The same tendency is deep within our lives today, sometimes hidden away, and at other times shallowly obvious. Human nature has a deeply rooted tendency to listen to the temptation to go its own way. The foundation of man's failure lies in his desire toward self-assertion and his determination to be independent of God. We desire to go our own way, to be our own master, but, as the lesson of Adam and Eve teaches us so plainly and painfully, when we listen to the voice of self-importance, we are doomed to experience discord and at some point we will certainly hit the wall – hard! D. R. Davies puts it well when he writes:

> Now in history we have to face the fact...that the human race through the individuals composing it, has willed itself out of the subordinate relation to God, with the fatal result that every individual becomes his own centre....Since we are all alike in wanting to be our own centre, we are irrevocably divided from one another. United in Sin, we become divided in everything else. This is the brilliant mess in which humanity finds itself, especially the progressive civilized humanity of today.[3]

As we confront the reality of life in this world, however, the difficulties involved in placing self at the center of our lives become very evident. In the present world especially, there are many things going against this whole uncomfortable idea of dying to self. Our society prides itself in earthly success, in the conspicuous accumulation of wealth, the perpetual striving for first place, and so forth. The elevation of self seems, in the world-philosophy of our age, the final purpose toward which everything else is somehow ultimately related. Our modern society has persuaded itself that natural goods such as wealth, possessions, physical health, and creature comfort are the primary justification of and even the very source of man's being. It has denied itself consideration of the necessity of renounc-

---

[3] W.R. Davies. *Down Peacock's Feathers*. New York: The MacMillian Co., 1946, pp. 10-11.

ing self for the sake of spirituality. Self-denial is thought to be associated with the world-negating attitude of medieval asceticism and the remnants of this same sort of outdated showy contrivance of early Puritanism. There is power, even deeply rooted within the most dedicated Christian, fighting against this notion of the repression of self. Man seeks to find a form of security through clinging tightly to the material and maintaining personal control, independence and autonomy, rather than through the invisible, the spiritual and the thin threads of faith and trust.

In order to better understand the necessity and centrality of dying to self in the kingdom of God we shall consider a few passages relating to Jesus and his earthly mission as they appear relevant to this point. The first passage is found in the Gospel of Luke 9:18-31, 36. The disciples, thinking that Jesus, in his kingdom, would bring about a sort of splendid or miraculous deliverance, were shocked when he informed them that he was to be a suffering Savior and that those who followed him must suffer also. In this poignant and arresting scene we have a simple but profound preview of what it means to be in the kingdom of God – it entails for us a dying to self just as it did for Jesus in his passion. Here we find couched within this solemn story a troublesome demand for a radical reorientation of the life – a life with the self no longer at the center. It is an enlistment of the inward man against the often subtle but ever steady pressures forced upon us by the world to put ourselves at the center of things. Our ordinary instincts flinch, as those of the first disciples assuredly did, as we face candidly the deep-rooted evils which most powerfully contradict this call to subordinate our all for the sake of following Christ. "Whosoever would save his life will lose it, but whosoever loses his life for my sake, he will save it." This was the Lord's watchword, and it ought to be ours as well. And when we look upon the life of Christ, through the eyes of trusting faith and divine wisdom, we realize that dying to himself was the key theme of his impeccable life. We realize, too, that we must emulate him in order to grow spiritually and win our own place in the kingdom of God.

The very first announcement about Jesus, as he launched his public ministry, was in essence a definitive declaration of his self-sacrificing mission. When John the Baptist introduced Jesus, he said, "Behold, the Lamb of God, who takes away the sin of the world!"

(John 1:29, 36). Again we see that Jesus' lifestyle is introduced to his own generation as a life of dying to self rather than living for self. How much insight John had into all of the profundities of our Lord's greater mission we do not know. We need not suppose that he had in his possession a full revelation concerning the mission of Christ, but we do feel confident that he did know that he had been confronted by the Messiah for whom Israel had been patiently waiting and that the Lord was to be the sacrificial Lamb of God. The Father had sent him into the human experience to deliver the world from sin by his atoning death. He was to sacrifice himself and everything he had, for a purpose and a cause beyond himself, finally dying to self in order mercifully to deliver men from the power of sin.

From this we may determine that the centrality of the Christian gospel is not the life of Jesus, nor his message, nor his works, but rather his death. This centrality is emphasized not only in the New Testament where its place is clearly seen, but in the Old Testament as well. In the first prophetic pronouncement regarding the coming Messiah in the Old Testament, we read: "He [Christ] shall bruise your [Satan's] head, and you shall bruise his heel" (Gen. 3:15). Even though his suffering is mild by comparison with the pain in the end that he will inflict upon the enemy, it is clear from this passage that he is to suffer injury from the experience. In addition, the great messianic prophecy of Isaiah 53 places great emphasis upon this same idea of the self-sacrificing Messiah:

> But he was wounded for our transgressions, he was bruised for our iniquities; upon him was the chastisement that made us whole, and with his stripes we are healed....He was oppressed, and he was afflicted, yet he opened not his mouth; like a lamb that is led to the slaughter, and like a sheep that before its shearers is dumb, so he opened not his mouth. By oppression and judgment he was taken away; and as for his generation, who considered that he was cut off out of the land of the living, stricken for the transgression of my people? (Isa. 53:5, 7-8).

The very center of the gospel of Jesus Christ is the cross. Who would argue with this proposition? The redemptive death of Jesus of Nazareth is the heart and soul of Christianity. As the Lord emptied himself and humbled himself, took upon himself human flesh and abandoned the glories of the heavenly realm, agonizingly giving his own life, so we also must have this same mind within ourselves (cf. Phil 2:5-11). We conclude therefore that in order to be like Christ and grow spiritually, we must die to self.

Jesus himself drew attention to the centrality of death in regard to his own earthly mission also. In speaking to Nicodemus, he said, "As Moses lifted up the serpent in the wilderness, so must the Son of Man be lifted up" (John 3:14; cf. John 12:32-33; Rom. 3:23-26; Heb. 7:27; Rev. 5:9). In this seminal text Jesus informs Nicodemus that what he has to tell men, as one sent by God from Heaven, is that he must be lifted up from the earth and experience death in order than man may have life. We understand that from his example that defeat and victory, suffering and glory, are particularly to be tied together in one's life. In order to be raised to new life, we must first die, just as Jesus showed himself willing to do. As the glorification of Christ came through the humiliation of his death, so the glorification of the Christian into true Christlikeness also comes through death – in this case death to self.

We must underscore the fact, though, that Jesus' death was absolutely unique. His death was substitutionary, suffered on behalf of others, and has infinite value because of who he is – God! In this one sense at least there could never be another death like his. He died once for all men and once for all time. Nevertheless, his death is one that we must, in our own human and rather feeble way, emulate. We, too, must die a death to ourselves. The first disciples died to hearth and home, calling and profession. We are called upon to die to our old lifestyle. Irrespective of one's situation in life, Jesus calls us to die to self and bravely enter a new world which is filled with substantial risks, of suffering, rejection, and those that have to do with our own peculiar cross to bear. In this manner, we die a death similar, at least in some small way, to that of Jesus.

In Luke 9:22 we read the following words of Jesus: "The Son of man must suffer many things, and be rejected by the elders and chief priests and scribes, and be killed, and on the third day be raised." Three fundamental things stand out in bold relief in this passage. They are: (1) rejection, (2) death, and (3) new life. Our Lord was to be rejected, then killed, and finally gloriously raised to a new life. His rejection and death unavoidably preceded his resurrection to a new life. What is so striking about this is that Jesus assures us that we will face the same kind of things as his faithful disciples: "If any man would come after me, let him deny [rejection] himself and take up his cross [death] daily and follow me. For whoever would save his life will lose it; and whoever loses his life for my sake, he will save [new life] it" (Luke 9:23-24). To take Christ seriously on these matters involves subordinating and even rejecting self and the things which the world values with such intensity, and doing this will most certainly in the end cause us to be rejected by the world. This does not mean, however, that we are to, as it were, pursue rejection and suffering simply for their own sake. Rather it means that we are to put Christ first and the natural consequences of this extraordinary choice will bring the disciple face to face with his or her own cross. To put Christ first may not spell physical persecution or actual martyrdom, but it could very well entail rejection and suffering over a period of many years and in a variety of different circumstances. But, as the case of Jesus so well illustrates, our rejection of the world and its reciprocal rejection of us, must precede any real and meaningful resurrection to a new life in Christ.

If we were to leave aside our belief in the uniqueness of the death of Jesus Christ and somehow purge it from our memory, we would be guilty of heresy of the worst kind. If we were to minimize his death, or liberalize it, we would rob it of its special nature and substitutionary character. By the same token, if we forget the necessary death of self in our relationship with Christ, or minimize it, or liberalize it, then we rob ourselves of the capacity to enjoy true spirituality and all we are left with is a life of sterile orthodoxy. If we fail to take seriously this obligation to die to self, we will in fact wither and die spiritually. As disciples, we must make a clean break with our previous way of life; otherwise we may find ourselves fully committed to a new set of doctrines but miss out on the recreated life. We may enjoy religion to some degree, live morally right, but be void of any spiritual depth or strength. The sad truth of the matter is that this has, in reality, happened to a great number of Christians who no longer "get much out of religion anymore." Such folk certainly need to ask themselves, "Where are the sacrifice, the pain, the cross-bearing, as well as the joy and peace, in my life?" The answer is that it is there for those who have experienced the discomfort, pain, and trouble which grows out of one's dying to self and living for Christ.

Christian discipleship was never meant to be an easy undertaking; and if it is genuine, it will not be easy now – it will call upon us to die. For the first disciples it involved physical danger and for some it even spelled martyrdom. During some of the darkest periods of history it meant death to several individuals, men like John Huss, Hugh Latimer, Dietrich Bonhoeffer, Paul Schneider, and others. Schneider, sentenced to death in the Buchenwald concentration camp in July 1939 by Hitler's SS troops, wrote to his wife, "Those who still want to avoid suffering...had better take care lest they be rejected among men and cast off by God." From this we realize the truthfulness of the statement, "Discipleship means allegiance to the suffering Christ, and it is therefore not at all surprising that Christians should be called upon to suffer."[4]

Our Lord applies the necessity of dying to self in a very concrete way in Luke 9:26, "For whoever is ashamed of me and of my words, of him will the Son of Man be ashamed when he comes in his glory and the glory of the Father and of the holy angels." It is possible by deliberate choice or manner of life for us to deny that we are followers of Christ. We think immediately of Nicodemus. He was well-to-do and comfortable and rather naturally shrank from the troubles, anxieties, and dangers of an open discipleship with Jesus. At this point in his life, he loved self and the opinion of the world more than he loved the Lord. Whenever we say "No!" to the Lord in an effort to win acceptance in society and with the world, we move a step closer to destroying ourselves spiritually. If we are unwilling to suffer with Christ, we shall not be glorified with him. Paul puts it in this manner: "if children [of God], then heirs, heirs of God and fellow heirs with Christ, *provided we suffer with him* in order that we may also be glorified with him" (Rom. 8:17). On the other hand, if we reject conformity with and acceptance by the world and die to the desire to center our lives in self, then and only then will we experience resurrection to a new life. Nicodemus later came to this realization, as did the apostle Peter after his repeated denials. It was the power of Christ working in men who died to self in order to live for their Lord that transformed dispirited and powerless men into a force that changed society and the prevalent culture, and ultimately al-

---

[4] Dietrich Bonhoeffer. *The Cost of Discipleship*. New York: MacMillian Publishing Co., 1946, p. 101.

tered the history of the world. And, what is more, this same power is available to us.

It may be necessary at this point to clarify further what we mean by this uniquely Christian demand of discipleship which encompasses this notion of dying to self. When we speak of dying to self, we do not mean an absolute negation of self as such, but a negation of self as evil. Some erroneously insist upon self-negation and world-negation in a sense quite different from that which is embraced at the heart of Christianity. They mistakenly require an absolute renunciation of self and of the world as a whole. Christianity, however, regards the self and the world as being essentially good since they constitute elements of the creation of a good God: "And God saw everything that he had made, and behold, it was very good" (Gen. 1:31). What the Christian faith condemns is the twisting and perversion of the self by sin and its idolatrous clinging to things in the world. Consequently, Christianity calls for a negation of the egoism of self and its perverse tendency to find its highest good in the world. Dying to self means therefore, dying to the corrupt human ego, dying to the irascible perverse desire to center one's attention and concentration upon the things of this doomed world.

As we reflect on this concept of life, let us again take note of the centrality of the death of Christ to his mission. Death, as foreign as that idea may be to our own way of thinking, was central and fundamental in the life and mission of our Lord and must come to be just as central and fundamental in the lives of his disciples. Discipleship is to be closely connected with the passion of Jesus Christ. Without the presence of such suffering in one's life there can be no real discipleship. Yet as we reflect honestly on our lives, we are made keenly aware of just how little emphasis we ordinarily place on dying to self and living for Christ. Let us ask ourselves a few explorative questions. How many of our thoughts, prayers, and everyday efforts do we center on the work of dying to self? Are not most of our genuinely strenuous efforts centered on removing the negative obstacles of life out of our way and making things easier for ourselves? Do we not pray and labor to remove these obstacles, rather than pray and work so that we might fully and faithfully develop the grace to walk in the steps of Jesus – steps which will no doubt with respect to the world involve rejection and death? We strain to live as disciples by taking the avenue of least resistance, rushing through and over and around the rejection and death to self that is so intrinsic to true discipleship. We want quickly to gain the goal of a new life in Christ without the aggravating distraction of jumping over troublesome hurdles of this sort. So, most of us take the easy route: we bypass altogether the most uncomfortable features of Christianity. We make an "end run" around this business of rejection of the material and sensual world and death to self and then we fitfully wonder where this great new life is that we have heard so much about from enthusiastic preachers and avid Bible teachers, and have read so much about in the pages of the New Testament.

Jesus equates discipleship undeniably and inextricably with the cross: "If any man would come after me, let him deny himself and take up his cross and follow me" (Mark 8:34). Suffering and rejection are two essential elements tied up with genuine discipleship, and we must recognize this or else miss out on the best that Christianity has to offer us. To take the Lord seriously will entail rejecting the things the world values and as such will cause Christians to be different from the world, hence, inevitably to be shunned and repudiated by the world. To fail to be serious in our discipleship is to water down our faith and turn it into a weak spiritual uplift that makes no real demands upon us but also has an inexpedient result: it bestows no real life upon its beneficiaries. The cross thus becomes a tragedy that occurred in the life of one man in history over two thousand years ago, but is not in any fashion whatever to be relived and repeated in our own modern lives. And so we find it difficult profoundly to believe; we do not seem to get much out of religion anymore; the worship activities of the church are not inspiring to our hearts and minds; God's commandments are difficult and hard for us to comprehend; and so it goes on and on, a vicious cycle of spiritual failure.

This is not, however, an inevitable conclusion to every life. There is another way. The answer to such difficulties lies in this simple but profound realization: only those who obey truly believe. If we find faith difficult to embrace with our whole heart and find the new life in Christ almost entirely absent in any really substantial way from our existence, then we will simply have to face up to the fact that we may not be bearing the cross that the Lord prepared for us to carry. It is possible that we are trying to keep back a part of our lives to ourselves. Remember the frightening story of the couple at Jerusalem who "kept back part" of what they promised to give toward the Lord's work (Acts 5:1-3)? Their selfishness and the lie they conspired together and told to the Holy Spirit led to disastrous consequences for them (Acts 5:3, 5, 10). Lying to ourselves about our commitment to Christ is no better than what this couple did! In order to correct this missing element we may have to be confronted by an uncomfortable but essential truth. Jesus put it in the following terms: "So therefore, whoever of you does not renounce all that he has cannot be my disciple" (Luke 14:33). We must be exhorted by this radical command to expeditious action and firm obedience. We must recognize that the real reason for our failure is not that we have embraced a faulty or confusing religion; rather, the problem lies with us and our own sometimes tenuous application to what we know. It is our own lack of obedience to the call to bear the cross and die to self. As was the case with Peter when he deigned to walk on the water with Jesus, we must first leave the security of the boat and walk on the water in faith and obedience before we can believe and live as the Lord meant for us to live and believe (cf. Matt. 14:22-33). Only those who obey believe. Any other position will lead to spiritual failure because it is void of spirituality and life.

We must realize, too, that this dying to self is not a once-for-all-times act which we can perform and then get on with our lives, but a *daily* commitment (cf. Luke 9:23), as was suggested earlier. True, as Christians, we are justified by the saving blood of Jesus and our past guilt is gone forever with salvation which we have come now to enjoy as a present-day reality in our lives. But solid commitment goes along with all these marvelous benefits. This commitment is underscored in an intensely practical manner by Jesus when he says, "If any one comes to me and does not hate[5] his own father and mother and wife and children and brothers and sister, yes, and *even his own life*, he cannot be my disciple" (Luke 14:26). This practical, ordinary, run of the mill life that we all live is ground zero for practical Christian living is where we must, on a daily basis, reject self and die to self. We must come to grips with the simple truth that most of us will

---

[5] This verb "hate" is the Greek present indicative active tense and means "continue to hate" or "continue to love less." It reflects a continuing or daily action.

not have to face death, or ostracism, or persecution, but rather the less dramatic, though often more painful and challenging, struggle against evil within ourselves and in our God-hating society. Most of all, we will have to confront the struggle against our own assertive ego and its selfish and demanding desires in the arena of our own hearts. Albert Schweitzer put it in these words:

> He speaks to us in the same words: "Follow thou Me!" and sets us to the tasks which He has to fulfill for our time. He commands. And to those who obey Him, whether they be wise or simple, He will reveal Himself in the toils, the conflicts, the sufferings which shall pass through in His fellowship, and, as an ineffable mystery, they shall learn in their own experience who He is.[6]

We live in an alien world that is the way it is because of man's rebellion against God. In our relationship with Jesus Christ we are not totally free from the unfriendly and unwholesome elements of this world, for they remain as warring powers within our sometimes divided souls. The apostle Paul fought this same nasty battle and characterized it in just those chilling terms (cf. Rom. 7:15-25), and we are no in sense superior to him. The reality of sin's persistent presence and virulent power is vividly manifested in our lives when we attempt to die to self and make a concerted effort to place self in the background. It is not merely that our natural impulses are hard to restrain; it is that they have been perverted by sin. The poverty and pettiness of our own little desires, problems, and sometimes twisted convictions seek to rob us of the wealth and splendor which are vouchsafed to us in Christ Jesus. When we are liberated from the heavy burden of such, foolish trifles, we are then free to bear the cross of Christ without inner distraction.

One of the most astonishing current ideas in the religious world is the outlandish notion that we can enjoy the benefits of Christ's salvation without accepting the challenge that we are to die to self. In a sense we can say that we have given the word away at wholesale prices. We have been led to believe that there is such a thing as a quick and easy discipleship – a discipleship without cost – which is in fact the broad way that leads to destruction. This easy cross-less

---

[6] Albert Schweitzer. *The Quest of the Historical Jesus*. A.C. Black, Ltd.: London, 1910, p. 401.

discipleship that has captivated the hearts so many of us has also hardened us into persistent disobedience, for when we hear Christian teaching that is foreign to our lifestyle or merely to our liking, we tend to close our hearts and minds to the very thought that such teaching might be true or even determinative for our faithfulness to God. This resultant cross-less discipleship devoid of spiritual demand or divine prerogative, has deceived and weakened us to the point where we have virtually lost the power to live a life of authentic discipleship and sacrificial obedience. This brings us back to our original premise. Take it or leave it: if we have the desire to know the dynamic reality of true spirituality, we must "take up our cross daily." To use our mental and physical capacities in an intentional effort merely to make ourselves respectable and loved by the world is not to be viewed only as an unfortunate directional choice in life, but it is to revolt against the One who created us and thoughtlessly to end up in dismal failure and perhaps even utter ruin. To die to self, however, entails a change that happens *in* us. It is a transformational change, a change of such a radical kind that it can only accurately and definitively be described in terms of a process of dying and being born again.

Discussion Questions

1. Describe in your personal daily life how you might apply the New Testament command to "die to self" in relation to discipleship.

    _____

    _____

    _____

    Comment: The centrality of the Gospel is not the life of Jesus, nor his message, nor even his works, but rather his death.

2. What is the difference between Jesus' "dying to self" and my "dying to self"? _____

    _____

    _____

3. Does "dying to self" entail a total self-negation and world-negation on my part as a disciple? Explain. _____

_____

_____

4. Explain this statement: "Only those who obey believe."

_____

_____

_____

V. From Death to New Life

Up to this point in our study we have spent a good amount of time in discussing the importance of dying to self in the life of the disciple of Christ. Jesus Christ demands that his followers die to self, deny self, and take up one's cross and die daily (cf. Luke 9:23). As death was central in the life and mission of our Lord, so it must be central in the life of his disciples, for Jesus said, "A servant is not greater than his master. If they persecuted me, they will persecute you" (John 15:20). When an individual decides to follow Jesus and rejects the ways of the world, a natural result of this decision is that the person so inclined will be hated and rejected in the same way that Jesus was. Dying to self and living for Christ and others over time will make the disciple so much like Jesus that the world will come to hate the Christian as much as it hated Christ.

To center our thoughts on death and that alone, however, would be downright depressing not to mention the fact that it would be missing the whole point of our new life in Christ. It would inevitably cause us to fail in teaching the good news of the kingdom of God. After all, in what sense would a concentration on death be considered "good news" to anyone? The life and mission of Jesus resulted in persistent rejection by the world and intimate experience with death, but it was also much more than merely this. Jesus' rejection and death were only preparatory to what has come to be recognized by Christian thinkers as the single greatest historical event in the history of the world[1] - his victorious physical resurrection to a new life. In

---

[1] This statement that Jesus was a real person in history is the exact opposite of the concept enunciated by liberal theology which speaks of the *kerygma* – the idea that we make Jesus the resurrected Lord when we preach him! Nothing could be further from the truth. We do not effectively

like manner, as his disciples, we too will find that if we are willing to live a lifestyle of rejection by the world and death to self, we also will be truly resurrected to a joyful new life. We can immediately begin to savor the powers of the age to come and be a joyful partaker of the glory that is to be revealed. As Paul says, "If any one is in Christ, he is a new creation; the old has passed away, behold, the new has come" (2 Cor. 5:17).

Dying to self entails a death to the habitual practice of sin and the result of such spiritual death is a new life, a life genuinely devoted to Jesus Christ. Paul wrote in Romans that "We were buried therefore with him by baptism into death, so that as Christ was raised from the dead by the glory of the Father, we too might walk in newness of life" (Rom. 6:4). Baptism after the New Testament order affords the believer participation in Christ's death, burial and resurrection. Identified with Christ in his death and resurrection, the Christian shares a new life and the very spiritual vitality of the risen Christ (cf. 1 Cor. 6:17; Col. 2:12-13). This change, which takes place in the newborn Christian, is not merely one of disposition but also one of lifestyle. Obedient believers are removed, as it were, not only from the flesh and the world, but also from the destroying power of sin. They are like individuals who have been buried in the tomb with Christ and now live in a new state of spiritual existence; they are a new creation. Re-enacting the death, burial, and resurrection of Christ in baptism, the Christian enters into the possibility of a decisive new life, quite new and utterly separate and distinct from the old. The Christian dies to sin, according to Romans 6:1-12, and is made alive to God. It is not that Christians are no longer subject to the possibility of sin, for they must fight the battle with the flesh to the end (1 Jn. 1:8-10), but that they are no longer slaves to sin. In Christ they are set free, sanctified, and bound to him, dead to sin and alive to God in Christ (Rom. 6:11-22). As Jesus died in history and once and for all was dead to the world and sin, so now the Christian is called in faith to count himself dead to his past practice to sin – at this present moment in history. The Christian dies now, not in an unreal, far-off world of religious mysticism, but dies in the here and now, in this world at the moment of his or her baptism. At baptism, then, we die to self

---

make Jesus the Christ when we preach him. He is the Christ whether we preach him or not!

and are then victoriously raised to a glorious new life, a new life that is real and that is *now*!

This new life is not delivered to us through some perceived experiential translation into a new dimension, or in a magical or mystical fashion. And surprising as it may seem for some who ever look to the future, neither is it to be found in a faraway millennium or even in eternity – it is now! Our nature is renewed by effort, by an effort of the power of Jesus Christ, and by our own confidence and trust in his ability to energize us and ultimately re-create us. Even the verb Paul uses in describing the new life, "walk," points to the fact that we must on our own part put forth serious effort. To "walk" (Rom. 6:4) requires a certain amount of earnest and persistent effort on our part, and it also presupposes a shining new goal ever before us. In baptism, God has bestowed upon us not only a new life, but also his life-giving Spirit (cf. Acts 2:38) to enlighten us with a vision and empower us with a constant motivation along with the strength and ability to "walk." And in our struggle with earthly passions and human infirmities, we are made constantly aware of this power within which aids and enables us to overcome these challenges. Dying and being raised with Christ in Christian baptism is a form of outward evidence that we are no longer abiding in our former sinful state of existence, but are transferred by God's invigorating power into the new life. We are no longer said to be "in the flesh," but rather "in the spirit." We are newly created beings with the Holy Spirit as our new life principle. Saved out of an old sinful life, we now enjoy a new and better one. We have left behind the old world of disheartening ineffectiveness. Raised above the limitations and strictures of the former natural self and the world which once held such fascination for us, Christians now belong to the Lord and begin their walk in a happy state described as "newness of life."

This transition from death to new life is difficult for us to comprehend in its fullness. We grasp for ideas and concepts to help us to explain or somehow define this new Spirit-empowered life and inwardly may even wonder if the apostles ever fully grasped its implications. One thing is clear enough though: the apostles were certain of the fact that through obedient faith in Christ, a man was radically empowered and integrally changed. Paul, for example, found this true in his life and could therefore write with perfect confidence, "I have been crucified with Christ; it is no longer I who live, but Christ who lives in me; and the life I now live in the flesh I live by faith in the Son of God, who loved me and gave himself for me" (Gal. 2:20). He is saying by this demonstrative and potent proclamation that even though he is obviously still living in the same old physical body, his life is not the old life it appears to be outwardly, but is deeply rooted and firmly grounded in a new life of faith, governed from within by Christ. Christ is now the sole meaning of life for the apostle. Every moment is passed in conscious dependence upon him to whom he continuously looks for everything.

The apostle Paul also knew of countless men and women who, in becoming Christians, were possessed with a new kind of life (one of which he writes about in 2 Corinthians 12:1-4). Here is a power that is not to be the exclusive possession of the privileged few – the kings and prophets and priests. Rather, it is a power that is to be given to all who are in Christ. The prophet Joel assures us of the general nature of this precious promise: "And it shall come to pass afterward, that I will pour out my spirit on all flesh; your sons and your daughters shall prophesy, your old men shall dream dreams, and your young men shall see visions. Even upon the menservants and maidservants in those days, I will pour out my spirit" (Joel 2:28-29; cf. Acts 2:17). Paul saw individuals transformed at the very center of their being, heart, soul, and mind. This transformation is one of the grand mysteries of the Christian faith, but it is also a reality and the revealed power of the Spirit of God at work in man's broken and sinful nature, renewing it in the image of God.

Thus, there is, according to the pledge of the new covenant, a radical new power actively at work within the world. Old forms, doctrines, and ideas will gradually but certainly die as the fulfillment of God's promise is steadily realized. "I will put my law within them, and I will write it upon their hearts" (Jer. 31:33), is first appropriated and then manifested in individual lives. This promise of power, given again by Jesus to his disciples (cf. Acts 1:4-8), is not mere human enthusiasm, natural reasoning ability, the general enlightening influence of God, or even the influence of the word only. It is a gift, a spiritual impartation from God. It is so universal in its expression and application that Paul denied the title of Christian to all who did not possess it and experience its directing influence: "But you are not in the flesh, you are in the Spirit, if in fact the Spirit of God dwells in you. Any one who does not have the Spirit of Christ does not belong to him....For all who are led by the Spirit of God are sons of God" (Rom. 8:9, 14). This power is intended to be a revolutionary force in the lives of all disciples and provides the impetus which moves them from death to new life.

If we are honest with ourselves, we are well aware of our bondage to self and sin. We do not need to be convinced of it. It is like a ball and chain that we have dragged behind us every step of the way in life before the Lord unburdened us. To overcome this, we may have tried all possible methods and devices to win our own deliverance from such bondage, but we have striven to little or no avail. In the past, the more we have struggled toward perfection through a "list-keeping" type of righteousness, or the more we give in to a "libertinistic" way of life, the more we have come to realize our utter helplessness in our unredeemed state. So we have been moved to ask and plead, "How do we overcome such a sinful, iniquitous, ungodly nature? How do we tap into the power of God, attain to his free gift of salvation, and come to enjoy his mercy and grace within our pitiful lives?" In essence, we cry out as did Paul, "Wretched man that I am! Who will deliver me from this body of death?" (Rom. 7:24).

Again and again we have emphasized Paul's ever present stress on the need to be immersed in water, buried with Christ in baptism (cf. Rom 6:4; Gal. 3:27; 1 Cor. 6:11; Titus 3:5; etc.). Yet this baptism was meant to be something much more significant and certainly more meaningful than the mere assent to or participation in a religious ritual. In responding to the invitation to Christian baptism, the believer acknowledges that Jesus has come from God, that he has a divine right to rule over his life as Lord and Master, that his life must be ordered by Jesus' teachings, and that he must die to self and live for Christ as did Paul. In all probability, however, most of us who profess Christ today have been baptized into Christ with the prosaic, perfunctory, and insipid confession, "Jesus is the Christ," when it should have been the promissory confession, "Jesus is my Lord." In other words, we must come to understand that we are confessing not so much that Jesus is the Messiah (although he most certainly is and ought to be confessed as such), as the principle fact that he is our only Lord and Master. This latter confession accentuates the fact that genuine Christian discipleship represents a life of perpetual loyalty and absolute surrender of self to Jesus as Lord. Discipleship involves adherence to the person of Jesus Christ and lifelong fellowship with him. The resulting life that we live is not adequately described as a form of hero worship akin to what which we might pay to a famous person but a surety of true commitment and a heartfelt obedience to the Son of God as Lord of our life.

There are few individuals within the western world today who do not believe that Jesus is the Son of God (even though secularism is growing more and more prevalent in our own day). But there are very many indeed who do not believe that Jesus Christ is the Lord of their lives, even within the church. Why do we say this? Simply because so many who profess to be followers of Christ continue to live in such a way as to reflect their inward conviction that they maintain lordship over their personal lives and that he has no say at all in the matter. At the very moment such individuals seemingly agree to follow Christ by submitting to baptism, they show the shallowness of their conviction and their apparent lack of willingness to follow him by making up their own rules almost daily: "I will follow you as the Son of God, providing it does not interfere with what I desire to do as lord of my life." This is the sort of "commitment" that makes discipleship so unutterably hard for us and spirituality an empty void rather than an empowering influence in our lives.

When we desire earnestly to possess that abundant life in Christ and fully to enjoy that mighty spiritual power within, then and only then can we receive such gifts by means of that process of which we have spoken so frequently: dying to self and rising to walk a new life with Christ as Lord and Master. We must make a clean break with our previous way of life which was centered in self. God wants to give us a marvelous gift out of his fullness, but he cannot give anything at all to us while we are distracted and busy with our own interests. We must first allow Jesus to be Lord and Master; then will follow spirituality and abundant life.

In giving us the Holy Spirit as our new life principle, God is truly granting us the much needed power to rise to new life from death to self. The Spirit is the pledge of the abiding presence of Jesus Christ and of our fellowship with him. Through this Spirit, God reveals to us his wisdom (1 Cor. 2:6-10). We are taught and brought into remembrance of all that Christ did and said on earth (John 14:26) and guided into all truth (John 16:13). The apostolic wisdom has become our own, and the apostolic remembrance has become ours also. What they knew we now know; what they remembered we now come to remember through their vivid recollections. The result of this is that we are enabled to walk in the Spirit and be assured of a constant fellowship with God in Christ: "There is therefore now no condemnation for those who are in Christ Jesus. For the law of the Spirit of life in Christ Jesus has set me free from the law of sin and death" (Rom. 8:1-2).

One additional note needs to be made in relation to this new life. It is not to be a life of sheer passivity or resignation. The Christian's life involves much more than a passive reception of the Holy Spirit and, in consequence of this acceptance, the Spirit's working in the individual's life. There must be a positive striving on the part of the receiver to conform to the image of Christ, and that should be the ready result on the part of all Christians. Christians are admonished by Paul "to grow up in every way into him who is the head, into Christ" (Eph. 4:15). There must be a progressive moral conformity to the character of Christ to such an extent that the very genuineness of our relationship to Christ will be determined by what we accomplish in the body. And with this effort comes the all-important promise: "I am with you always, to the close of the age" (Matt. 28:20).

Certainly we recognize that after the new birth we remain human, made in the image of God, yes, but still humans burdened with weaknesses and failings. God, however, deals with us as such and aids us in growing spiritually. He urges us to actively yield ourselves to him.

> Do you not know that if you yield yourselves to any one as obedient slaves, you are slaves of the one whom you obey, either of sin, which leads to death, or of obedience, which leads to righteousness? But thanks be to God, that you who were once slaves of sin have become obedient from the heart to the standard of teaching to which you were committed, and, having been set free from sin, have become slaves of righteousness. I am speaking in human terms, because of your natural limitations. For just as you once yielded your members to impurity and to greater and greater iniquity, so now yield your members to righteousness for sanctification (Rom. 6:16-19).

Do you, simply by reading it, sense the force of action present in this passage? According to Paul, rejection, death, and resurrection to a new life are now behind us and we are ready to be used as God's instruments of his divine will. As slaves to sin, we had to keep on sinning, but now, enslaved to God, we can continue in righteousness. The powers of God within make us alive to our responsibilities as citizens in the kingdom of God. This indwelling power of the Spirit lifts us out of the narrow and selfish life and unites us and all our sympathies with God and neighbor. This Spirit so received is the dynamic source of our Christian life and conduct.

Discussion Questions

1. The new life in Christ is not future only, but a present-day reality. Describe this truth as it has been and is being revealed in your walk with Christ._____

   _____

2. How does baptism play in the life of a disciple? Is it a mere ritual or does it have spiritual implications beyond this?_____

   _____

3. How might a Christian betray his confession that "Jesus is Lord of my life"? _____

   _____

VI. Living the New Life

In our study thus far, we have discussed the need that we all have for salvation from sin, and in one sense from self. We discovered that it is the work of Christ on the cross that makes it possible for one to become a child of God. Once we respond to God in faith,[1] we are raised from death to a new life as a child of God, a member of the kingdom of God. We also found out that such a new life is not to be one characterized by either legalism or libertinism, but one of spirituality and response to God. This type of lifestyle, in turn, involves the internal necessity of love – love manifested toward God and man. Such love on our part involves something much more profound and selfless than a libertinistic attitude such as was apparently manifested by some of the Roman Christians in the first century (cf. Rom. 6:1). This love involves, as we have previously noted, a dying to self, a sacrificing of one's very life (cf. Matt. 16:24; Luke 9:23-24).

The change involved in becoming a new creature in Christ is of such a radical kind that it can only be described in terms of death and dying. But, as we explained earlier, to center our thoughts on death and that alone would be to fail in our understanding of the good news of the kingdom of God. It would be tragic to suppose that the salvation offered in Christ means merely the settlement of past sins and the death of self, and these things alone. Precisely as Jesus' own rejection of self and physical death on the cross were only preparatory to the greatest event in the history of the world, his resurrection and glorification (cf. Phil. 2:5-11), so, too, we must come into possession of a new life or else we will have missed out on the finest aspect of the Christian experience. This new type of existence

---

[1] Faith is belief in God and Christ, which implies assent to the will of God, and the attitude of trust, loyal obedience, and persevering faithfulness.

will reveal itself not in passivity or resignation, but in a dynamic life of power and fullness.

God and Christ are not merely interested or solely concerned with the settlement of the account regarding our past sins and getting us into the body of Christ. These are of course important, but not all-important. They are as much concerned with our present and future life as they are with the business of putting the past into the past. After first securing our forgiveness and reconciling us to God, our Lord then empowers us with his Spirit so that we can overcome the present evils in our day-to-day existence. This new birth, or new life, we have in Christ, is meant to be an all-inclusive way of life and living. It is meant to embrace not only our acceptance with God, but also our progressive liberation from the tyranny of self and the happy restoration of harmonious relationships with our fellow man. The barriers we have erected between ourselves and God, as well as our fellow man, due to hatred, contempt, and lack of concern, must be removed and replaced with better motives as well as more pleasant practices in the future. Only in the presence of this type of inward and outward reconciliation can we ever hope to approach that abundant new life promised to us in Christ. Thus, due to the life, death, and resurrection of Jesus Christ, we have the possibility of a new life in the here and now and the prospect of life eternal in heaven. And due to the power of the Spirit of Christ within each baptized believer, we can be set apart from the evil power of self and be unified with God and neighbor in a continuous fellowship of peace and love.

In order to be practical, however, we must frankly ask ourselves if this new way of life is truly possible. And if it is possible, how are we going to develop and live in this new way? What can we begin to do? At the introduction of this study, we saw that we cannot simply wait, or stand idly by hoping for some sort of religious experience that will mystically change us from a spiritual caterpillar to a butterfly. Nor can we gain such an end by completely immersing ourselves in a rigid system of works, legalistically, methodically, and heartlessly striving to keep the commandments. We shall certainly not attain it by giving ourselves completely over to a free, libertine lifestyle either. We do not gain Jesus' abundant life by means of any of these man-centered avenues. How then do we live in this new manner? Once again, the way to begin living the new life is in just the same fashion in which we became Christians – an intensely practical way. Let us meditate upon this question and see whether if we study further we may not find that God has an answer for us.

The apostle Paul reveals the simple practicality of this new way of life when he writes, "For while we are still in this tent, we sigh with anxiety; not that we would be unclothed, but that we would be further clothed, so that what is mortal may be swallowed up by life. He who has prepared for us this very thing is God, who has given us the Spirit as a guarantee" (2 Cor. 5:4-5). What the apostle is saying here is that we recognize the abiding afflictions and often painful limitations of this present earthly existence. However, even though life is sometimes quite unpleasant, we are not at all anxious to lose our physical lives but would desire rather to put on a spiritual body without facing the cruel sting of death. Paul further assures us that, in preparing for eternal life and in developing us toward spiritual maturity, God gives us the Spirit as a guarantee that a transformation process is now at work in us. God's strength is sufficient and his power is made perfect in our weakness (cf. 2 Cor. 12:9). These are the spiritual resources amply supplied on God's part that enable us to triumph in our new life in Christ. We do not, cannot in fact, transform or recreate ourselves through our own strength alone; it is the abiding presence of the Spirit of God within that enables us to face the challenges of life with confidence and by his divine power makes us sure of our reception of this new life in Christ. It is the Spirit of God within which enables us to triumph: "Thanks be to God, who in Christ always leads us in triumph" (2 Cor. 2:14).

With these things in mind, let us look once more at on Paul's memorable words: "I have been crucified with Christ; it is no longer I who live, but Christ who lives in me; and the life I now live in the flesh I live by faith in the Son of God, who loved me and gave himself for me" (Gal. 2:20). Here we are informed that Christ really lives in us and, living in us, he has promised to bring forth fruit in us just as the vine bears fruit in the branches (John 15:1-5). This then is the complete picture of what our union with Christ becomes when we die to self, are buried, and arise to walk in newness of life. A vital connection with the life, death, and resurrection of Christ is fundamental to genuine spirituality and fruitfulness. Abundant life is available to us when we are united with Christ and begin to draw from his strength.

Jesus gave a solemn warning to his unlearned disciples, "Apart from me you can do nothing" (John 15:5). In the earliest stages of our own spiritual development, we might have accepted such a statement with a healthy dose of indifference. For in such immaturity we would tend to speak out of a false confidence, fully believing that this is so: "We can grow and develop spiritually by our own efforts at learning and doing God's will." And so we started out confidently on the road of self-centered list-keeping and legalistic observance of our understanding of God's commands, ignoring the necessity of the grace and mercy of God. We had the comfortable feeling that we could, with determination and strong effort, achieve spirituality on our own terms and by our own effort. Faced with any temptation and given enough time and sufficient effort, we could eventually overcome through our own strength of will. Realistically speaking, however, we are quite likely to find ourselves at a dead end when we have tried this route under our own strength and based on this misguided approach to our religion. It is so difficult to realize our goals, to resist temptation, to attain that spiritual maturity we desire so intently but seems ever to be out of our reach. It is in the midst of such persistent and humbling failures that Christ confronts us with these biting but empowering words: "Abide in me, and I in you. As the branch cannot bear fruit by itself, unless it abides in the vine, neither can you, unless you abide in me....for apart from me you can do nothing" (John 15:4-5). This passage reveals to us that the greatest experience of that abundant life found in Christ can be realized as we feed on the nourishment supplied by the Spirit of Christ, the invigorating Vine of our life.[2] Spirituality comes only as a result of a living, life- sustaining relationship between Christ and us, as his dependent disciples. This relationship is precisely what dying to self and living for Christ provides.

Many of us fail to grow spiritually because our conception, our idea, our consciousness of Christ is smaller than our world. By con-

---

[2] A branch taken from a vine may live a few hours by feeding on itself, but it soon dies because it has no ability to re-supply itself with energy. In the same manner, we may live a little while on our own abilities, but soon we, like the branch, start to wilt and die spiritually. We must be united with Christ in a very meaningful way if we are to live and continue to live abundantly.

trast, a spiritually maturing Christian has his faith rooted in an awareness of Jesus Christ as a living contemporary in his personal day-to-
day existence. So if we would live the new life in Christ to its fullness,
we must appreciate the validity of Christ as our contemporary. Jesus
Christ is not just a figure in ancient history; he is not a mere nostal-
gic memory from the pages of an old book we once read, nor is he
merely a person we encounter in the Scriptures. He is the Christ that
we can know in a present tense experience, a Christ immeasurably
larger and more powerful than our world or anything we will ever
experience within it. He is the Christ that lives within who makes it
possible for us to say, "He spoke to my fathers; he speaks to me. He
taught my fathers; he teaches me. He saved my fathers; he saves
me. He guided my fathers; he guides me." We must be concerned
with what he is doing with us and in us today, and remove from our
minds the comfortable but false notion that he merely acted in the
lives of some first century Christians and is with us today only through
his recorded sayings set forth by inspired penmen. Listen again to
our Lord's animating and heart-bestirring promises: "I will not leave
you desolate; I will come to you" (John 14:18), "I am with you always,
to the close of the age" (Matt. 28:20), and "I will never fail you nor
forsake you" (Heb. 13:5). We need the power of Christ in our lives in
the here and now and he assures us that he is with those who love
and trust him in every age. This central note must be sounded again
and again so that we do not lose its preciousness.

This same biblical truth concerning the living relationship of
Christ and his Spirit to the Christian is emphasized several times in
Paul's letter to the Romans. Beginning with Romans 5:1, the words
"through Christ" are used several times in the epistle: "Therefore,
since we are justified by faith, we have peace with God *through* our
Lord Jesus Christ." In Romans 7:24-25 we read, "Wretched man that
I am! Who will deliver me from this body of death? Thanks be to
God *through* Jesus Christ our Lord!" And in Romans 8:37 we read,
"In all these things we are more than conquerors *through* him who
loved us." Again and again in Romans, Paul repeats this epic phrase,
"through Jesus Christ our Lord." He speaks of the new life of the
Christian and all that this life entails. Without Christ and his Spirit,
we would remain in bondage to the powers of sin and of the unre-
strained self. But when Christ becomes our Lord, he brings an end
to the dominion of such destructive and enslaving powers. We are

no longer held in their encircling grip. The power of the resurrected Lord in us will begin to bring forth the fruits of the new life from us in the liberty of our new-found freedom. No Christian can gain spiritual maturity due to the virtue of his own merit or his ability always to obey and remain faithful to God's will alone. It is rather on the basis of what Christ has already done at Calvary and is now doing within our lives. That "peace with God" (Rom. 5:1), that deliverance "from this body of death [sin?]" (Rom. 7:24), and the ability to be "more than conquerors" (Rom. 8:37) are possible with us now because of the new relationship we have with Christ and his Spirit. With this relationship there is now a way possible for us to achieve the spiritual maturity designed for us by God's redeeming activity in Christ. With the transforming power of the Spirit of Christ within, we can have the ability to live this new life.

The thing that makes the difference in our quest for a fuller depth of spirituality is the indwelling Spirit of Christ. It is not to be from our own strength that we gain this spiritual maturity; rather we receive, upon our death, burial, and resurrection in baptism, the indwelling and empowering Holy Spirit of God who makes possible the realization of this goal and ideal. This work of the Holy Spirit within is brought out for our understanding with great force by Paul in Romans: "If you live according to the flesh you will die, but if *by the Sprit* you put to death the deeds of the body you will live" (Rom. 8:13). Here the Holy Spirit is specifically introduced as the agent of the power and person of Jesus Christ. We do not possess the strength for a new life in Christ, but with the power of his Spirit within, we can "put to death the deeds of the body" and so realize the transformation to new life in Christ. Through Christ we have actually been freed from the power of self and all the claims self has made upon us in the past. Walking in newness of life (Rom. 6:4), the Spirit permeates all of our life and sets the old, outward self back to the past where it belongs. And we must understand that we have access to this power within now, for our Lord assures us, "I will not leave you desolate; I will come to you" (John 14:18).

But the one thing that will inevitably undermine such a new life in Christ is our love for self – that desire to center our lives on self. Such an emphasis results in the impossibility of gaining that spirituality in Christ that we can possess. Through Christ we have been delivered from sin and the unbridled self, and for this very reason we must fight against any attempt that the assertive self makes to re-conquer what it has lost. While in this physical body, we still live in the continuous struggle with the flesh and the very real possibility that we can again fall under bondage to self. Paul speaks of his own personal encounter with this ongoing inward resistance in Romans 7:23. He graphically describes a "law in his members" which is at war with the law of his mind. Such a fight, however, is not waged by the Christian alone and in his own strength. Were this so, it would be no better than a "lost cause." We "live in the Spirit" and "walk in the Spirit," and therefore are encouraged by the knowledge that we are enabled by this Spirit to "put to death the deeds of the body" which strive to overcome the life in the Spirit. This is God's promise: "To all who received him, who believed in his name, he gave power to become children of God" (John 1:12), "[f]or all who are led by the Spirit of God are sons of God" (Rom. 8:14). Thus we are confidently assured that in Christ we are freed from the overbearing self that we may enjoy joint participation in this new life granted to us by God.

The promise of the Holy Spirit to be our ever-present companion is given again in 2 Corinthians 13:14, "The grace of the Lord Jesus Christ and the love of God and the fellowship of the Holy Spirit be with you all." The power to live the new life in Christ and the power which sustains the individual Christian comes through this promised indwelling Spirit. The essence of this promise is that we do not have to face the loneliness and frustration of fighting a solitary battle in striving to grow toward spiritual maturity; rather we have the Holy Spirit assisting us in creating out of our old self a new man. This spiritual power was gradually but effectively working within the early disciples, transforming ordinary men like Simon Peter, that previously weak, Christ-denying disciple, into the rock that he eventually became, and re-creating the fearful and scattered disciples into that dynamic force that struggled against a stubborn culture until it turned the world upside down. In spite of the fact that several times Jesus put a small child in the midst of his disciples and urged them to humble themselves as that child, Peter and the others remained at first proud and self-confident. Yet a few years later they achieved an impressive level of maturity. We cannot help but notice this maturity in Peter's references to the need for humility as he pens his epistles to other developing saints. Our Lord taught the disciples to love one another, but John had the reputation of being a hard-nosed "son of thunder" due to his personal severity toward others (cf. Luke 9:54). Yet again, in a few short years we see, with some considerable astonishment, this same "son of thunder" writing about and practicing that great mark of the mature disciple of Christ – love for one another (cf. John 13:34-35). What brought about this difference in the lives of these disciples? In our view the answer is simple. It was the power of the Holy Spirit as he entered into their unremarkable lives and changed them from within, making of them some of the most notable people who ever graced this planet. And this same power and influence is available to us. We find in the scriptures not a group of super-Christians laboring together, but a rather ordinary group of men and women – very much like ourselves – motivated and indwelt by the power of the crucified and glorified Lord, the Spirit of Christ. The Holy Spirit is a reality in the lives of God's people, indeed, the reality for which our very existence as sons of God is continually dependent.

From studying the lives of the early disciples, it is evident that the Holy Spirit is to be identified with the Spirit of inward renewal which characterized these extraordinary men. This is the process whereby the life of the newborn Christian is increasingly made into conformity with the life of Jesus Christ. But this is not an overnight *regeneration*. It is a lifelong *renovation* that is, as it were, the growing up of the Christian, the outworking in thought, word, and practice of the life that is receptive to the Spirit. It is the sanctification that is not only the product and consequence but also the goal and end of justification. We refer to Simon Peter again. He wrote his first epistle about thirty years after the resurrection of his Lord. In this epistle he revealed a growth and humility he did not possess during his early years with Jesus. By this time Simon was a remarkably different and noticeably more spiritual man. This reveals to us that Peter did not change overnight, as if it were by a single event or happening, rather his spiritual growth came about through a gradual process over an extended period of time. Several years after the resurrection of Christ, Peter fell back into some of his old ways, denying the Gentile Christians full access to fellowship (cf. Gal. 2:11-12). Paul had to withstand him to his face. The point is: growing into Christ-likeness takes time. It is not an overnight experience. This doesn't mean, however, that the Spirit is not working in us just because we don't see growth as fast as we would like to see it in ourselves or even in others. The Spirit worked in the life of Peter, the fisherman apostle; he is also working in us.

We need, at this point, to again emphasize that the work of the Holy Spirit within our lives does not mean that we have no personal involvement in the matter of developing spiritually. Our lives are not on "autopilot" with the Holy Spirit at the controls. Granted, we cannot succeed in our own energy, or effort, or through works alone, but there must still be a personal and effective response from us. There must be evident within and without the putting off of the works of the man or woman we once were prior to the denial and death of self. Because of the fact that our old self will not die easily, there are warnings in the scriptures not to contend against the indwelling Spirit but to open up the heart and life to him and his power. We are to live and grow, to be vibrant and positive, and to be filled and compelled by the Holy Spirit. In the words of the inspired penmen of God's word, we are to be "filled with the Spirit" (Eph. 5:18), to avoid grieving the Spirit (Eph. 4:30), and even more seriously, to make sure we do not douse the flame of spirituality or "quench the Spirit" (1 Thess. 5:19). Failure to work and cooperate with the Spirit in renewal will result in a stifling of the power of God at work in us to recreate us into the image of God's Son, Jesus.

An illustration of how we must respond to the Holy Spirit is given in a situation from the life of Mary, the mother of Jesus. In Luke 1:26-35 we read of an angel coming to Mary to inform her that she was to give birth to the long-promised Messiah. After this encounter with the angel, there were two possible responses Mary could have made. First, she could have rejected this purpose of God due to her love for her husband, Joseph, and the fear of what he might have thought about all of this. She might have been concerned with what others might think or say about her. But Mary did not take this route. On the other hand, she could do as she in fact did. She accepted the Lord's will for her life in spite of whatever misgivings she may have had relative to other matters. She became a vessel to be used in the service of the Divine: "Behold, I am the handmaid of the Lord; let it be to me according to your word" (Luke 1:38). Mary gave herself to God, by choice, for him to do with her what he purposed. She believed the promise from God, yielded her mind and body to his will, and the result was that all of heaven and earth were changed when Jesus was born. In a similar manner, we are in much the same situation as was this humble virgin of Galilee. We have a magnificent and thrilling promise of a new life possible for us in Christ, a life potential beyond all of our imagining. However, we cannot achieve such a life under our own power or by our own strength. Neither is God going to do it for us by overwhelming our powers of resistance. We must humbly submit ourselves to him. If we are to live in the reality of this new life in Christ, we must, like Mary, submit our lives to God's direction and care. There must be from us a constant trust and faith in his leading. We must say with Mary, "Let it be me according to your word." When we do this, then and only then will we realize the goal the Lord has set before us, that of being "changed into his likeness from one degree of glory to another" (2 Cor. 3:18).

This, then, is what the New Testament teaches about spirituality in the life of Christians. When we place our trust in Jesus Christ and, without mental reservation, commit ourselves to him, then the Holy Spirit enters into our lives. The Spirit is sent by God into our hearts making our bodies his dwelling place: "And because you are sons, God has sent the Spirit of his Son into our hearts..." (Gal. 4:6). And "do you not know that your body is a temple of the Holy Spirit within you, which you have from God?" (1 Cor. 6:19). The Holy Spirit is not the natural possession of all men, but rather comes into our lives through the act of dying to self and being resurrected into a new life in Jesus Christ. Those who commit themselves to this way of living are thus governed by the Holy Spirit and have the possibility of an abundant life in Christ, a fullness of life which is illumined and empowered by the indwelling Spirit of God. We have not just been given a fresh start and then left to work out our own life in Christ with a little assistance from the scriptures and fellow Christians. Rather, we are given a new life, and our task is to live this new and fresh life in the strength of the Spirit and in the direction of Jesus Christ.

Living in the Spirit does not mean, however, that from now on we are exempt from the possibility of sinning. On the contrary, in some ways the conflict of the soul with its nemesis is intensified, but *a way of victory now has been made available to us*. The battle is indeed intensified, for as Paul cautions us, "the desires of the flesh are against the Spirit, and the desires of the Spirit are against the flesh;

for they are opposed to each other" (Gal. 5:17). This is a daily battle and the common experience of all who are within the body of Christ. Daily we encounter the power of sin as it strives to drag us down into the mire, but we are now conscious of another more powerful force pulling us upward toward Divine holiness and the ultimate purity of heavenly perfection. And the more we, like Mary, surrender our lives to the indwelling Spirit of Christ, the more this Spirit will work and move within us to create in us a Christ-like character. Paul speaks to this subject of developing into spiritual maturity when he intones that "we all, with unveiled face, beholding the glory of the Lord, are being changed into his likeness from one degree of glory to another; for this comes from the Lord who is the Spirit" (2 Cor. 3:18). It is not only that we have to strive to live like Jesus, but also that Jesus by his Spirit has promised to come and joyously take up his abode with us.

Thus, the freedom from sin that we can have in Christ does not consist in having no master. It is not a type of libertinism or limitless freedom to do whatever we desire, but rather it is having a new, gentle and loving Master, one who understands us completely. It is important that we understand the reality of our situation. We are a slave, either to self or to Christ, to the flesh or to the Spirit. From the moment we submit to the Spirit, we have a new life and enjoy a new freedom from sin. This freedom, however, is not license to do as we please but a type of joyous "slavery" to the good, and that is the highest conceivable freedom or life the human spirit can ever know. And how do we come to enjoy this life? We cannot gain it by attempting to cultivate directly the virtues set forth by our Lord (what some would call list-keeping), and we certainly will never come to know it by libertinism. We gain this new life by graciously welcoming the Spirit of Christ into our hearts and lives. When we do this, Jesus promises that "the water that I shall give him will become in him a spring of water welling up to eternal life" (John 14:14). When that stream begins gently to flow in our lives as a perpetual inward spring, then we also will begin living the new life which the Lord promised for us.

Discussion Questions

1. What guarantee does God give us in relation to spiritual development when he sends his Spirit to dwell within our lives?_____

_____

_____

2. Is Jesus Christ a living contemporary in our lives or a historical figure only? Explain._____

_____

_____

3. How do you see the work of spiritual regeneration and renovation at work in your life? _____

_____

_____

VII. The Spiritual and the Natural Worlds

As we are well aware, living the new life in Christ is not without its problems. One of the first of these problems is that of living spiritually in a naturalistic generation. We are to be "aliens and exiles" (1 Pet. 2:11) in a world where man has become the prey of a peculiar kind of sin called "naturalism." More and more the world is being viewed by many as being purely external to God, as being wholly profane and de-divinized. All naturalistic philosophies have in common the belief that "nature is all the reality there is." There is no divine origin or spiritual meaning to life. Man, history, life, everything is to be interpreted in terms of the physical nature. God and all the accompanying spiritual realities have become distant and even absent in the world's way of life. Man is part and parcel of nature and is to be explained wholly in terms of natural laws and processes. The popular appeal of the death-of-God theologians is evidence that many in the world live in an atmosphere of the absence of God, or naturalism.

This naturalistic attitude in the world can also infiltrate the thought-world of Christians to the extent that Christians can lose the reality of their spiritual lives. In order to combat this, we must understand that the world is not what our generation says that it is. For example, a life of prayer and thankfulness to God has absolutely no meaning and significance whatsoever unless we live in a spiritual world with a spiritual God who objectively exists and acts. We must understand the presence of a spiritual reality that is nonetheless that which is nearest of all, present throughout the universe, and in human life itself. As humans, we are primarily spiritual beings, created by God, and in whom God is spiritually manifesting himself in and to so that he might realize his external purposes.

This fact is illustrated in a powerful manner on the Mount of Trans-figuration, Matthew 17:1-8. This event on the mountain happened in the real, physical world and, all the while, life in this physical world continued on during this event. What Matthew gives us here is a su-pernatural, spiritual event happening in relationship to the physical and natural world. And we realize from this that the spiritual world is not a far-off cosmos, but a reality that exists in our present world and in our own time – a reality that is just as true and real as is the natural world which we experience daily. In the scene at the Mount of Transfiguration, the spiritual world was at the top of the mountain. We know that we are physical beings living in a natural world, but we know, too, that we are spiritual beings living in a spiritual world. It is only when we allow our spiritual vision to become blurred by those who make an idol of the material world and its values that we begin to doubt this.

A second example of the reality of the spiritual world in the midst of the physical world is found in the Gospel of Luke. Writing about our Lord's appearance to his disciples on the road to Emmaus, Luke records these words: "And their eyes were opened and they recog-nized him; and he vanished out of their sight" (Luke 24:31). The literal translation of this passage is, "He became unseen to them." Luke did not say that Jesus was no longer there, but that they could no longer see him. The fact of the matter is that Jesus is always pres-ent, always with us within the spiritual world which surrounds us: "I am with you always, to the close of the age" (Matt. 28:20). At the very center of the Christian's life should be an intense awareness of the spiritual. Our lives should be spiritually intoxicated to the point that we are embraced on all sides by the reality of the divine. This is not to be an otherworldly spirituality either, but rather the realization of the reality of the spiritual world and the divine presence in the daily round of human tasks and at the important junctures of human life as well as in periods of worship.

The reality of the existence of these two spheres, the spiritual and the natural, in our world is seen in the Old Testament also. Af-ter he made the covenant with God at Mizpah, we read that "Jacob went on his way and the angels of God met him; and when Jacob saw them he said, 'This is God's army!' So he called the name of that place "Mahanaim" (Gen. 32:1-2). The word "Mahanaim" means "two camps" and refers to the fact that Mahanaim was a place of double encampment. It was the camping place for Jacob's family, as well as the camping place for the angels of God. The point of this incident is to suggest to the reader that one camp is as real as the other. And throughout Jacob's life there is presented to him the reality of this spiritual world. Jacob saw angels on a ladder in his vision at Bethel (Genesis 28:10-17). On another occasion the Lord spoke to him and told him to leave the house of his father-in-law, Laban, and return to his own people (Genesis 31:3). Near the end of his life, when he blessed his children, he said, "The angel who redeemed me from all evil, bless the lads" (Gen. 48:16). The striking thing that makes itself apparent in all of these stories from Genesis is the fact that this man of God had so many enlightening encounters with the unseen spiritual world. This reveals again the duality of the world that we live in – a world that is both truly spiritual on the one hand and obviously natural on the other.

A final example from the Old Testament which reveals this same truth is found in 2 Kings 6:16-17. In this section of scripture, Elisha is suddenly and hopelessly surrounded by his enemies and the servant who has accompanied him is understandably terrified. Surprisingly, Elisha was confident and calm in the face of this sudden terror for he realized the presence of God and so was not in any wise panic-stricken like the servant. With the servant it was a very different story, for he was a man who did not realize or appreciate God's presence. So to comfort and assure the frightened fellow, Elisha said, "Fear not, for those who are with us are more than those who are with them." Now under the circumstances, this must have sounded utterly absurd to the servant. But it did not continue so for long because Elisha prayed for his enlightenment, "O Lord, I pray thee, open his eyes that he may see." Next we read that "the Lord opened the eyes of the young man, and he saw; and behold, the mountain was full of horses and chariots of fire round about Elisha." The point of this story also is that there is a spiritual world surrounding all of us which is invisible to the human eyes. This is not to say that it is unreal either. It is just as real as the natural world that we do see. It is there in spite of our blindness to it. An unsighted man in our world may not be able to detect the presence of a tree 100 meters out in front of him, but that does not mean it is not there. He may never touch it with his hand or bump into it, but that still does not prove it is not there. It only means that he does not have the sensory perception to detect its presence. We cannot detect this spiritual world either, but we cannot therefore deny its reality or explain it away.[1] We cannot see the air that surrounds us, but it is still there in great profusion – and it is comprised of the stuff of which the physical world is made! Still we cannot see it. What we need to appreciate in every hour of our lives is that we are also just as truly and actually living in the presence of God and of the spiritual realities of this world as were the ancient patriarchs and prophets. Then we need to take comfort and genuine consolation in this fact (cf. 2 Chron. 32:7; Psa. 34:7; 68:17; Dan. 7:10).

As we think further on this relationship between the natural and the spiritual worlds, we can begin to understand the importance of Jesus' figure of himself as the vine and his disciples as the branches bearing fruit (cf. John 15:1-5). For too long we have tried to explain the Lord's portrait of this relationship as a mystical, otherworldly, abstract teaching. If we can view it in some way other than in terms of the naturalistic opinion of the world, however, we will come to realize that this concept is not really so strange after all. The scriptures insist that we live in a world that is both spiritual and natural. If we find this concept difficult to accept, then the spiritual realities of our life in Christ, such as communion, prayer, and the presence of Christ,[2] are illusory and without palpable foundation. All that results from following this idea to its necessary conclusion is a faith that is no more than a psychological and sociological tool. The truth of the matter is that we do not have to rely on such things alone. We have the presence and dynamic realities of the spiritual world available to us. They represent a dynamic presence which sets the word of God aflame in our hearts, has the potential to kindle individual disciples into action and strengthen those same disciples with power in the

---

[1] Cf. Joshua 5:13-15, which details Joshua's encounter with an angelic commander of the Lord's heavenly armies; see also: Num. 22:21ff.

[2] This promise is more than influence, for influence alone would provide us with little real comfort – we yearn for the person. The promise is that Jesus is here with us as friend and Savior. This may come to us slowly: first Christ as a figure in history, then a Light to guide our life, then a personal Savior, and hopefully, finally a Presence and Companion in life.

inward man. As Paul assures us, "You are not in the flesh, you are in the Spirit" (Rom. 8:9).

If there is a spiritual world, and such a realm must exist for the reality of the Christian faith rests upon the actuality of the existence of a personal God and the factuality of the presence of a spiritual world - then the Christian is a person who lives and abides continually in this spiritual realm. Again, according to God's word, the world is made up of two aspects or spheres of reality, the spiritual and the natural. One we cannot see with our physical eyes; the other we can see if we are sighted. Our present generation denies the existence of the unseen part of the world and the persistent temptation in this present cultural and ideological environment is for us to go along in order to get along. But to be a New Testament Christian implies that we must continually and truly live in both of these dimensions of the real world – the natural *and* the spiritual. However, it is so very easy for us to be won over to the world's way of thinking to the extent that most of our lives are lived as if the spiritual aspect of our present reality did not exist and did not represent any part of genuine existence. The Bible says that we are born again into a new way of life, yet most of us live as if the only true reality was the physical naturalistic world until the arrival of an indefinite future at the time of our death or the sudden in-breaking of the second coming of Christ. Our horizons have been seriously narrowed by our continuous past experience with the material world to the point that we are restricted only to naturalistic considerations as regards our thinking processes. Our idea of life as we perceive it has come to be based upon what we see, what we feel, and what we can touch. This is true to such an extent that we possess an impaired spiritual vision. This attitude toward life is simply unscriptural and wrong. The word of God speaks of this spiritual/natural world as a genuine reality. It is imperative, therefore, that we realize and appreciate the genuineness of this spiritual aspect of the world for the scriptures are said to provide us with all things necessary for us to have "life and godliness" (2 Pet. 1:3) and furnishes us completely "for every good work" (2 Tim. 3:17). The scriptures were written to man, informing him of the true nature of this world (both the seen and the unseen), of himself, and of his physical and spiritual needs. The scriptures also tell man how the world functions and how we are to function within it.

We need to learn well this important lesson for our lives today. The temptation is powerful in the face of worldly tensions to give in to the urgent and at times brutal realities of the immediate natural world versus the seemingly distant and indistinct spiritual one. Too many times we allow the tension and turmoil of our lives to make our faith in the spiritual realm seem like only a lovely and lofty, but wholly impossible, dream-like fantasy. We must never forget how and under what historical challenges the Christian faith began. It started in a world brutally mastered by superior military might and governed by the irresistible forces of the inimitable Roman Caesars. Into this harsh environment, however, came a small group of people who believed sincerely in a redemptive spiritual message and the genuine existence of a spiritual world amidst the tension of living in a totally different and antagonistic world. In the end, who was it that survived to influence all of the ages that followed? Was it Peter and Paul, or Nero and Domitian? As powerful as these Roman rulers appeared to be at the time, thankfully they have had precious little influence upon the ages that have followed. In contrast, Peter and Paul changed the world and in the West have influenced every generation that followed after. The Christians of the first century saw themselves as living not in one world, but two. They experienced as a result of this "double-vision", not just the tension and anxiety of this present world alone, but the effervescent power and a persistent vision of a world beyond this one that is both unshaken and unshakable. As the writer of the letter to the Hebrews expressed it: "We have this...sure and steadfast anchor of the soul..."(Heb. 6:19).

If it is true that these two worlds to which we have alluded exist in space and time, then what are the real and practical implications of this for our everyday lives? The first implication is an intriguing one, and is set forth by the apostle Paul in his first epistle to the Corinthians: "For I think that God has exhibited us apostles as last of all, like men sentenced to death; because we have become a spectacle to the world, to angels and to men" (1 Cor. 4:9). The Greek word for "spectacle" (*theatron*), which means "theater," is a word employed to describe a place for public assemblies, like the ancient Roman theaters. What Paul is emphasizing here is the truth that Christians are, as it were, on display and are continually being observed by the spiritual and physical worlds which surrounds us. In a sense, they are the audience that watches the unfolding drama in our lives. We do not merely live unto ourselves as we so often perceive of our daily trek though this world. If the Bible is true, then, there are spiritual intelligences who know about and are deeply concerned with our welfare: "Are they not all ministering spirits set forth to serve for the sake of those who are to obtain salvation?....Therefore, since we are surrounded by so great a cloud of witnesses, let us also lay aside every weight, and sin which clings so closely, and let us run with perseverance the race that is set before us" (Heb. 1:14; 12:1).

This same emphasis is made again by the apostle Paul when he writes to Timothy, "In the presence of God and of Christ Jesus and of the elect angels I charge you to keep these rules..." (1 Tim. 5:21). Timothy is never alone. He is observed by God, by Jesus Christ, and by the angels. As Christians, we also are never alone. We can go on and on with many other splendid biblical examples of this truth. Christ informs us that the angels in heaven rejoice over one sinner who repents (Luke 15:10). In the book of Job we are informed that the spiritual world was concerned with the life and activity of this great patriarch (Job 1:6-10). The spiritual world is a reality now. It is a reality that transcends the reality of the natural world of everyday life. It is not a long way off but present reality. Our part in it is not unimportant. We are being observed and our life here in this world is not to be viewed only as a natural life but also a spiritual life.

This concept of the spiritual world is not to a sufficient extent a reality in most of our lives, however. Today the spiritual world as a meaningful reality is entirely absent or very remote from the horizons of the everyday life of people in modern Western societies. We seem to manage to get along quite well living absent a belief in the reality of the spiritual world. In a world that is war-torn, cruel, brutal, filled with hatred and in denial of much that Jesus taught and died for, we have a rather natural tendency to attempt to solve our problems with our own powers, and frequently do not look beyond them for help or support. Our whole lifestyle is often so immersed in naturalistic thought that we forget that other world which remains invisible to our eyes and ears. And so – out of sight out of mind – we often ignore the fact that Christ is with us now, that his Spirit is within us, that we are to bear fruit as the bride of Christ in the here and now, and that this present life is one of spiritual as well as physical reality. We do not deny the importance of doctrine, but if our doctrine is coupled with and energized by naturalistic powers only, we can neither mature in Christ, nor acquire that goal of spiritual maturity that we so meaningfully desire.

Have you ever wondered about the mystery of an airplane as it faithfully keeps its course through the heavens day and night through all kinds of weather? The secret of "this ship of the skies" lies in the fact that it moves in two worlds. On the one side is the plane itself, the air it rides on, the clouds it penetrates, and the visible world around it. But there is another world that only the pilot and his bank of gauges knows about, invisible, intangible, working its magnetic fingers and unseen radio waves on the plane's compass and direction-finding equipment and ultimately providing guidance even in a blinding storm or thick cloud cover. We are like this, too. One part of our world of perception is natural, physical, and visible. The other is immaterial, invisible, and intangible. In order for us to enjoy the full richness of the life the Lord came to share with us, we must lift ourselves up into this spiritual sphere and realize its power, the true potential of its faith, the magnificence of its ideals, and the true glory of its visions of beauty and right. Christ did not come into this world, teach a small band of disciples and then die on the cross leaving us to struggle along in this physical world under our own powers alone. He places within our easy reach remarkable spiritual powers, and we see in real and practical terms such forces at work in many lovely, elevating, and genuinely Christlike people about us. We have seen good people endure the darkest of times enlightened by the promises of Holy Scripture. We have witnessed men and women of God who have kept alive their devotion and have continued to direct their gaze upward to that higher spiritual world in spite of the most tragic of circumstances. In this world they have found freedom from the trouble and despair of the physical realm, arriving at a wholeness of life that is hard for the atheist and the secularist to explain.

We also need to know that we can have fellowship with the powers of this spiritual world in this life. Indeed, we also long to enjoy freedom now from the troublesome bonds of sin to a greater degree than we ever previously thought possible. One need only take a look at the lives of great men of God like Moses, Abraham, David, Daniel, Peter, Paul, and Jesus Christ to catch some idea of where such dynamic fellowship ultimately leads. These individuals did not live in an ivory tower, attempting to escape this present evil world, but faced inevitable real-world trouble – tremendous turmoil – between the brutal and the beautiful, the evil and the good, the actual and the possible, the temporal and the eternal. This was their sometimes unhappy and difficult lot in life. Yet they resolutely and steadfastly refused to surrender their belief in the higher spiritual realm to escape such tension. These men all believed in that higher and qualitatively better spiritual realm and maintained this belief in spite of the anxiety and strain which resulted. It is fully within our power to have this same faith. We are convinced of this. In fact, Paul assures us of this:

> So we do not lose heart. Though our outer nature is wasting away, our inner nature is being renewed every day. For this slight momentary affliction is preparing for us an eternal weight of glory beyond all comparison, because we look not to the things that are seen but to the things that are unseen; for the things that are seen are transient, but the things that are unseen are eternal (2 Cor. 4:16-18).

We will never, on this side of the "veil of tears," be able to attain a state of spiritual perfection in the sense of utter sinlessness, for that is not possible in this life. It is entirely within our reach, however, to move closer and closer with each passing day to genuine Christ-likeness than we ever dreamed possible. We can only attain this level of spiritual maturity, however, if we plug in to and utilize the powers that are available to us in the spiritual world. Our ability to live in the spiritual dimension of this world is real and altogether possible. When we do this, then prayer, worship, daily Christian striving, and deep inner spirituality will come to be living realities to us. Without an appreciation for these realities, human life is diminished and ultimately impoverished. With them, our life will move nearer to that fullness which God intends us to enjoy: "I came that they may have life, and have it abundantly" (John 10:10b).

It is imperative, in the midst of present and very troublesome turmoil and tensions, that we keep this spiritual realm of the Christian's life before our eyes and in our hearts as a present and attainable reality. We need Christ more than ever before to pass his kindly but stern judgment on our ways and to give dependable guidance to our course of life (cf. Matt. 6:25-34). It is precisely in the midst of a storm or while flying through a heavy cover of clouds that airplane pilots most need to keep the compass, radar and radio indicators true so that the airship may reach its final destination. In a very real sense we must do this also. In the storms of life we must keep our sights on the higher spiritual world where the power of God resides and keep ourselves locked on to the spiritual verities which make life even in this world truly worth living. We cannot endure successfully to the end if all we now see is this visible, tangible, shaken, and very broken world. Unfortunately, many Christians in our time live in unnecessary personal turmoil and agonizing anxiety simply because they fail to do as Moses did: "He endured as seeing him who is invisible" (Heb. 11:27).

Discussion Questions

1. What biblical examples can be cited which reveal the presence of both the spiritual and the physical worlds which surround us? _____

   _____

   _____

2. What are the implication within your life in relation to the biblical concept that Christians are on display and being observed by both heavenly and earthly beings? _____

   _____

   _____

VIII. The Christian's Commission – Demonstrate

Now that we are more fully aware of the duality of our world – one part natural and physical, the other supernatural and spiritual – and all the powers available to us in the spiritual realm, we are brought face-to-face with a challenging commission from our Lord. With the realization of the true duality of our world comes also a sobering responsibility, or commission, that being to demonstrate to our generation the reality of the spiritual world in the midst of this physical sphere in which we live and move about daily. It is intrinsic to the nature of the Christian faith to expand by a process of sharing, and the propagation of the faith is synonymous with the gospel itself. We cannot rest until the good news of the reality of our spiritual world is heard, believed, and appropriated by those for whom it was also created and to whom it is addressed.

Our world today is basically no different from the Assyrian, the Babylonian, or the Roman world of the Old and New Testament eras. There is no universal peace to be had for the individual, or for mankind in general, in our age anymore than there was in the ancient ages past. The reason why this situation exists is because many continue to live their lives in the natural realm of this world oblivious to that other plane of existence and with no recognition at all of the spiritual realities which are forever present and always available to them.

Certainly we realize that this ignorance on the part of man was not the original plan and is not the will of our Creator. On the contrary, God knows that our times need desperately the reality of the Christian faith, not because nothing else is available, but because there is nothing else sufficient. As human beings, we are immersed in the naturalistic world, yet we cannot live in true contentment by the naturalistic philosophy alone. We must rise into the realm of the spiritual in order to enjoy fully our present state, for man is more essentially spiritual than many of us may have realized. He thirsts for mystery, meaning, community, and even for some sort of spiritual praxis. God did not intend for the world to be a place that is lonely and empty for us, devoid of tangible proof or manifest evidence of the reality of the spiritual. We live in a temporal world where in the end change inevitably and incessantly alters everything we experience, but God has given us the eternal word as well as an ever-present guide who is "the same yesterday and today and for ever" (Heb. 13:8).

The Christian faith provides spiritual resources that can enrich and empower the lives of individuals and communities. In our spirit-starved age, people need such resources. The gifts of the Spirit - love, joy, peace, patience, faithfulness, and gentleness - are resources that can meet the needs of our time. Many would tell us that these resources are of no value in the present world because we need, above all, a practical lifestyle rather than one motivated by high-sounding "virtues". Many continue to prize the Christian faith due to its lofty ethical teachings or because of the impressive figure of Jesus Christ, skillful Master Teacher and unparalleled moral philosopher. Yet its spiritual side – prayer, worship, and the rest – is set aside as being impotent in the world of today. What we need, many say, is to develop the practical aspects of Christianity, not the spiritual aspects. Yet in flat contradiction to such thinking, great numbers of people are searching for some sort of "spiritual experience" and are rebelling against the very faith that ought to be providing it for them. This spiritual crisis of our modern society is a promising opportunity for us to bring to it the radical change that takes place in every life that is deeply and genuinely committed to Jesus Christ. Therefore, it is imperative that we assume our God-given responsibility of declaring to the world the reality of the rich resources that can be helpful in meeting the spiritual needs of our generation, indeed, of every generation.

A casual examination of the scriptures reveals that God designated Christians as his agents and burdened them with the responsibility of revealing to the world the realities of the Christian faith. This special task has a place of absolute primacy, and nothing else takes precedence over this. Inspired by God, the apostle Peter wrote to Christians, "You are a chosen race, a royal priesthood, a holy nation, God's own people, that you may declare the wonderful deeds[1] of him who called you out of darkness into his marvelous light" (1 Pet. 2:9; cf. Isa. 43:21). The Christian is to be a life-giving source, as was Christ, in that he will show forth to others, by life and word, the true reality of the God who makes the Christian what he is. Not that he will possess the spiritual graces available to him in perfection, but that he will provide living proof of that spiritual world which faith in Jesus Christ opens up to all men. In the laws of the spiritual universe in which we live, it is only by faithful evangelism that we can ever hope to see genuine revival in the hearts and lives of individuals. God did not have it is his plan that there were to be no concrete evidences of the reality of the spiritual blessings and powers we have in Christ.

As we have stated before, it is imperative that Christians believe in and embrace with the whole heart right doctrine. It is not sufficient, however, simply to believe the right doctrine or just to proclaim right doctrine. We must not only be right in what we do, but we must also be right in how we do it. Faith is not just a matter of the intellect. It involves the imagination and the emotions and, indeed, the whole life of man. What is the value of right and true doctrine if it is not manifested before the hearer in a right and effective manner? The Christian faith does not merely entail a belief in an event which happened long ago or a convincing doctrinal system composed of various truths; it is also a generous sharing in the spiritual experiences of the root meaning and power of that faith. How can we express to others in mere words the pleasing realities of the spiritual world which we claim surrounds us if we ourselves do not live a "supranatural" or authentically spiritual life? If our life is grounded in the natural world, if we live as if the physical world is all there is until the arrival of an unknown future time, then we are not going to be particularly effective in declaring the excellencies of God's mercy and grace to others who live after the same fashion. We do not mean to de-emphasize the blessings of eternal life by this approach. Eternity

---

[1] Greek – *aretas*, meaning "excellencies" or "perfections" of God.

will be totally spiritual, totally wonderful, but there are some things on earth that we will not have in heaven, and among those things is the commission, responsibility, and privilege of sharing with those outside a relationship with Jesus Christ the blessings and joys of the spiritual life available to us in this world.

As we demonstrate to the world the spiritual realities of the Christian system, however, we must avoid the very human temptation to center the source of our conduct in self-power. The apostle Paul admonishes Christians with these words: "I appeal to you therefore, brethren, by the mercies of God, to present your bodies as a living sacrifice, holy and acceptable to God, which is your spiritual worship" (Rom. 12:1). A Christian's faith is sterile if it does not produce a new quality of life, but this lifestyle enjoined by Paul is not in its entirety a human action whereby the will of God is fulfilled in us. Rather it is a demonstration demanded by God for his glory.[2] We are always tempted to believe that by buckling down and multiplying the number of our deeds of charity and our religious observances we will be pleasing to God and thereby merit his good grace. Contrary to this thinking, all ethical behavior on our part is nothing more than a demonstration, even though it is a demonstration that is both a necessity and an obligation. There is no such thing as the "building up" *by men* of an adequate ethical life, regardless of how much man may be attuned to the will of God. All human spiritual development is simply an occasion or opportunity to point to that which alone is worthy of being called beneficial action, namely the operation of God in the lives of men. Whenever individuals in this world see real spiritual power in our lives, there they also see the power of God at work in this world in and through us. Thus, all our human responsibilities, virtues, and good deeds in Christ are, as it were, set upon the edge of a knife. The man who practices and cherishes them must be prepared to see them not as self-achievements, but as the action of God in his life and thus demonstrate them to the world for the glory of God and the salvation of man.

Individual disciples are called upon to demonstrate to the natu-

---

[2] Recall again 1 Peter 2:9, "But you are a chosen race, a royal priesthood, a holy nation, God's own people, that you may declare the wonderful *deeds of him who called you* out of darkness into his marvelous light."

ral world that the supernatural, spiritual world is a reality, and that within this natural world is in evidence a new and spiritual world also. Christians are to do this individually, and we are to do it by revealing the reality of this spiritual and powerful world within our own lives. And it is imperative that we engage in such activity NOW! We can not do it in the past (if we have not already), nor can we do it in the future. We must demonstrate to our world now, at this point in history, that the spiritual world is as real as the natural. It would be a great tragedy and a gross injustice to the world for us to think that we can be all that God would have us to be while sitting quietly by, passively contemplating the exceptional honor and the pure excellence we personally enjoy in Christ, without sharing such with others who need it so desperately. The fact is that a failure to demonstrate our faith and love to the world results in the unavoidable decline of our own spirituality. Apart from the spiritual mission to demonstrate something distinctive and different, the Christian has neither real significance nor hope for long term survival. If we, as Christians, have nothing spiritual to contribute to the world, what footprint do we leave upon the sands of time? We are not socially, economically, or politically superior to others. What can we do in these realms that others cannot do, and perhaps do even better? If we fail to demonstrate that spiritual quality of life that belongs only to those in Christ, then we are doomed to wither away and die spiritually, as are those others to whom we are commissioned to demonstrate the virtues of Christianity. We must, therefore, submit to the rigorous discipline which has been set before us as out lot and our life. As light and leavening influences in the world, if we are committed to this cause, then we cannot help but demonstrate to the world the wonderful spiritual blessings available to all who live in Christ.

Why haven't we been more effective in the past with our demonstration of these verities? Why is it that we so often speak with the wisdom of *Time* magazine, or the realism of newspapers and radio and television? It is not because we do not have the truth of God, the power of God, and the word of God. Perhaps it is because we don't truly believe in the reality and power of the spiritual world ourselves. Maybe we have become so grounded in the naturalistic philosophy of our present secular age that we have been unable to overcome its powerful influence upon our own thinking. It could be that our minds have been focused too much on the world scene. How, then, do we avoid this situation? How do we bring ourselves to realize anew that we have the weighty responsibility of heralding the good news to others so that all families of the earth may be enriched with the spiritual blessings of God?

As in all other areas of Christian living, we cannot overcome our weaknesses and failure alone. We need the power derived from the One whom we may be presently denying – the Holy Spirit of God. The early disciples also needed this power. When our Lord commanded them to teach, or demonstrate, to the world the good news, he also told them to wait for the power of the Holy Spirit:

> While staying with them he charged them not to depart from Jerusalem, but to wait for the promise of the Father, which, he said, "You heard from me, for John baptized with water, but before many days you shall be baptized with the Holy Spirit....But you shall receive power when the Holy Spirit has come upon you; and you shall be my witnesses in Jerusalem and in all Judea and Samaria and to the end of the earth" (Acts 1:4-5, 8).

The Lord wants us also to depend upon him as the main resource for our spiritual energy. In essence, he challenges us: "Begin now and let the world see a demonstration of what the spiritual power provided by the Lord God can do when it works through you who trust in the Lord implicitly."

The early disciples were effective in addressing the needs of their world because they were filled with the power of the Holy Spirit on the day of Pentecost. If they gave themselves to the Lord's cause with reckless abandon, it was not because they had no use for or love of life; it was because life had become a most precious possession and they gave it back as an offering to Jesus Christ. Life had real meaning for them in Christ, and they were alive and powerful, filled with the Holy Spirit.

We realize, of course, that the early disciples enjoyed a special circumstance in that they were possessors of the miraculous measure of the indwelling Holy Spirit, but we cannot imagine that it was somehow a different Holy Spirit than the one available to Christians today. "Be filled with the Spirit" (Eph. 5:18) is a valid and present command addressed to us today as it was addressed to the Christians of the first century by Paul. The inner presence and power of the Holy Spirit is the spiritual birthright of every Christian. And it is by the help of this Spirit that we can be transformed into the very image of Christ and illustrate to the natural world the reality of the spiritual world which although it is invisible to the unaided human eye, nevertheless surrounds us. It may well be that our prior unsuccessful demonstrations to the world concerning the spiritual realities in Christ have proven ineffective because we have been attempting to demonstrate solely by our own efforts and in our own strength.

Why does the world continue to stand outside the fellowship of God through Jesus Christ? Why does the world seek substitutes in the form of alcohol, drugs, materialism, and so forth? Is not all this a symptom of the failure of Christians fully and victoriously to infiltrate their shattered world? Is not all this substitute-seeking a symbol of a deep void in the hearts and lives of men and women in our world? And is not the solution to such ills and voids easily within the reach of the hands of faithful disciples? We must demonstrate to the world through our own joyful existence the joys which are available to them in Christ. Our world is hungry for spiritual blessings. It is our duty and happy responsibility freely to share our rich spiritual life with our fellow travelers in this world.

Discussion Questions

1. How would you respond to a worldview that states that the spiritual aspects of the Christian faith are impotent in relation to our lives and that only the practical aspects of the faith are beneficial? _____

    _____

    _____

    Comment. Did the early disciples give their lives with reckless abandon because they had no use for life in this world?

IX. The Christian's Responsibility – Declare Salvation

Why is it so essential that Christians provide a substantive proof to the world as to the reality of the spiritual universe which, Scripture says, coexists with this present physical world even though unseen? Some sort of conclusive evidence is essential in order that we may declare to a skeptical world the necessity of the salvation of humankind that is available in Jesus Christ. And this is a declaration that is needed, not only for those outside the body of Christ, but also for those already in Christ, for we, too, need to be continually assured of our ongoing relationship with God. Christians continually stand in need of the strength derived from an assurance of forgiveness and a consciousness of reconciliation by a gracious and merciful God in the face of our persistent struggle with temptation and sin. The very purpose of John's first epistle was to pass on to disconsolate souls this greatly needed assurance: "I write this to you who believe in the name of the Son of God, that you *may know* that you have eternal life" (1 John 5:13). Eternal life in Christ, although a part of the "age to come," is also *a present possession* of the Christian who lives in an abiding relationship with Christ the Lord.

When we become Christians through faith and obedience to God's will, the Sacred Scriptures assure us that we stand justified before our Creator. The very center, as well as the climax, of the gospel is this justification and the strengthening assurance which grows out of our knowledge that God loves us beyond measure and gave heaven's most valuable treasure to secure it. The cross of Christ is evidence that God has not overlooked sin in our lives. The nature of our individual sin, its "exceeding sinfulness" as Paul would describe it (Rom. 7:13), is the very thing that cost Jesus so very dearly in the agony and suffering he endured and the very thing that cost God his Son. In Christ, however, it is the consistent testimony of the Holy Bible that individual sin has been punished and the obedient believer now stands justified in the presence of God. It is as though the person had never sinned. The account has been cleared. The slate is clean. The price has been paid. On the cross Jesus took all the punishment and guilt for sin, and what this means to the obedient believer is that there is no punishment or guilt for him to bear in this life or in the age to come. After the atonement, our heavenly Father, as the righteous Judge, declares that Christians are freed from the bondage and guilt of sin. All of this rests in the fact and work of God's Son upon the cross. Justification is the process whereby God brings a previously fallen and condemned humanity back into a proper relationship with him. The world desperately and urgently needs this good news. It needs to hear it and it needs to act upon it.

We must be careful here, however, to avoid the foolish mistake of declaring an easy justification, or cheap salvation, to the world. Easy salvation is really nothing more than false salvation. In the end it is only another way of condoning or taking lightly the true magnitude and awful consequences of sin. Sin is justified, but man is yet lost if his own sins are yet unremitted. It does not help or rescue a lost man; it actually harms him, for such counterfeit salvation is not genuinely helpful or even truly Christian. Too many conceive of God as an easygoing, grandfather-type, who looks down with an indulgent eye upon the faults and failures of his grandchildren, the sons and daughters of men. Yes, God is faithful and just to forgive, but such justification is made possible only because his Son bore our sins and took our place on the cross. The truth is that God does not view sin lightly, nor does he ever ignore it. The entire Old Testament is a testimonial to God's view of evil. It is a record of divine judgment upon human rebellion. He hates sin and one need only look intently and circumspectly at the cross to realize this truth. Yet this cross offers one the only way to be reconciled to God. His cleansing power is available freely and abundantly to mankind. When we first yielded to temptation and sinned, it must be understood in order for it to be genuinely appreciated that, it was that sin which helped nail Jesus to the cross of Calvary. Every other sin that we have committed had a part in the same ugly process. The good news is, however, that God in his providence and grace was not willing on his part that we remain in this helpless and pitiful condition. He has provided a way out. God has made provision for our salvation through the cross of his precious Son. This truth must be boldly and persistently declared to the world.

Viewing the cross in this light then, the well-informed Christian realizes two essential elements are involved in the justification process. The first is the harsh fact of divine judgment concerning our personal sin. At this point we are reduced to less than nothing as we encounter God in the person of the one truly Innocent and Righteous One who was cruelly abused and ultimately crucified, and thus paid the awesome debt of our sin. We are, however, in a sense to be identified with that crucified and cursed One who died on Calvary's cross. When we confront the awful reality of the cross, no doubt we are moved to say with Isaiah of old: "Woe is me! For I am lost; for I am a man of unclean lips, and I dwell in the midst of a people of unclean lips; for my eyes have seen the King, the Lord of hosts!" (Isa. 6:5). How vast is the gulf between the lofty spiritual being that is God and mere mortal man, even at his noblest and very best. We can never genuinely feel the degree of our personal inadequacy, or experience the putrid uncleanness of our lives from God's perspective, until we go back in our mind's eye to the foot of the cross. Only there do we experience the true cost of our sins.

But there is yet another word we come to know while standing at the foot of that "old rugged" cross. As condemned sinners, surprisingly we are also to be identified with that righteous One who was in every way pleasing and acceptable to God. The assurance of the complete forgiveness of sins and the removal of iniquity, wickedness, and unrighteousness from our lives was made possible through the saving work of God done at the cross. It is at this moment that God declares the obedient sinner righteous and once again in harmony and fellowship with him as in the beginning, before sin ruthlessly intervened and devastatingly disturbed the relationship. The reality which makes this all possible is the forgiving and cleansing grace of God which fits us and qualifies us to be his children. When the reality of this marvelous truth makes the God-designed impact on our lives that it was intended to, we will be motivated, nay compelled, without a moment's hesitation, to gladly proclaim this salvation to all peoples. Convicted of sin and made keenly aware of God's grace, we are ready joyfully to serve God. This same attitude of heart and mind was that which David appropriately demonstrated after his own fall from grace and subsequent repentance: "Create in me a clean heart, O God, and put a new and right spirit within me....Then I will teach transgressors thy ways, and sinners will return to thee" (Psa. 51:10, 13).

Justification must also be understood as being freely given to all individuals who respond to God in saving and obedient faith. The apostle Paul assures us that "there is no distinction; since all have sinned and fall short of the glory of God, they are justified by his grace as a gift, through the redemption which is in Christ Jesus" (Rom. 3:22-24). There are no degrees of justification – one is not more or less Christian, but a Christian indeed or not a Christian at all, solely on the basis of Jesus' work accomplished on the cross. In the realm of justification, the things which weigh so heavily with us as human beings – merit, achievement, inheritance, position – all count for nothing. Regardless of how well we may have fulfilled the requirements of the law, or how many times we may have found the opportunity to sit in harsh judgment of others, we are all in the same manner and by the same process equally justified before God. As there is no difference between men with respect to their characters as sinners, so there is no difference with respect to their receiving justification in Christ Jesus. By one supreme act, Christ broke the bonds which entrapped man in the practice of transgression and so freed him from the iron shackles of sin. In Christ there is a full life now and in the future, free from the fear of predictable failure, cleansed from the guilt of past sins, and loosed from sin's continuing domination. How imperative it is then that we as God's redeemed people declare the availability and richness of this salvation to the world!

There is, however, much more conceptually and practically to salvation than justification. Whereas justification is a past work performed by Christ on behalf of the Christian, the future for the Christian is glorification when Christ returns to resurrect the body and usher his faithful disciples into eternity. But Christianity is not just a preoccupation with the future; what about the present time? The present life of the Christian concerns the daily task of growing into

Christlikeness, or that process which is sometimes technically called "sanctification." The issues involved in what we describe as sanctification arise from the fact that justification means to *declare* righteous and not to *make* righteous. Sanctification, on the other hand, may be defined as the gracious work of the Holy Spirit by which he frees the *justified* sinner from the pollution of sin, renews his entire nature, and enables him to live a vital life as a Christian. It is the process in which the new life is given to the believer by the indwelling power of the Holy Spirit and the believer is thereby released from the compulsive power of sin and guilt. The richer meaning of sanctification lies not merely in separation *from* sin, but also in ones' relation to the living Spirit of Christ. The authenticity of the new life in Christ is determined by the genuineness of the believer's sanctification in the Holy Spirit. Sanctification, we might say, is the Christianizing of the Christian. It is the development of the abilities to the point where believers have the capacity to express love in response to hate, faith in the place of fear, peace in the midst of persecution, truth where there would otherwise be slander, strength when troubled by weakness, and trust when tempted to distrust and mistrust. Sanctification depicts a struggle, it is the striving within and without to make our whole lifestyle one which enables us to love God and serve our neighbor. In other words, sanctification is the living process where one becomes more and more like Christ in character and life style.

Earlier it was pointed out that there are no degrees of justification – one is not more or less a Christian, but a Christian or not a Christian on the basis of Christ's finished work on the cross. Such is not the case, however, as regards the matter of sanctification, for in our present life there are most assuredly going to be degrees of spiritual growth. Sanctification is not so much an act as it is a gradual growth process. Moreover, spiritual growth for the Christian is not a straight line process, nor does it develop on an unbroken, inclined plane. In real life, we are sometimes up and at other times we are down. Justification deals with our position with God in relation to his Son, so it is not possible to be justified in varying degrees. Sanctification, however, deals intimately with the power of sin in our lives and with God's intense and loving desire to bring us into communion with himself. Sin within our lives, on the other hand, has produced a separation or estrangement between us and God. The result is a perennial tension within our lives between the aggravating power of sin and the energizing will of God. It is this ever-present tension that produces the ups and downs in our spiritual lives. In fact, the greater one's spiritual growth, the greater and more persistent is the sense of one's sinfulness and unworthiness. We increasingly see ourselves in the pure light of God's perfect holiness and are abhorred by our own disgusting uncleanness (cf. Isa. 6:5). Yet, out of this comes an altogether salutary effect, as we increasingly realize the amazing depths of God's redeeming love. Paul experienced this, just as we do, as he pointed out in Romans 7:15-25.

We must also realize that sanctification, like justification, is a work of God's grace within our lives. We cannot, by our own efforts and without divine aid, attain the goal of sanctification. It is not produced by our own good works or intelligence. Rather, sanctification is the result of our response to the Lord's call to come out and be a separated people, dependent upon God to work this change in our lives. As time passes we will realize a more consistent victory over sin, a greater love for God, more power in prayer, and more joy in Christian fellowship. These things are not reasons for self-congratulation, either, but rather reasons to thank God for working and living in us, developing us increasingly toward the object of spiritual maturity.

From this we understand salvation to be a growing process developing from justification (a past experience), through sanctification (a present action), to glorification (a future reality at the second coming). This process is revealed by giving careful attention to the verb tenses used in passages such as Romans 8:28-30:

> We know that in everything God works for good with those who love him, who are called according to his purpose. For those whom he foreknew he also predestined to be conformed to the image of his Son, in order that he might be the firstborn among many brethren. And those whom he predestined he also called; and those whom he called he also justified; and those whom he justified he also glorified.

This same truth is revealed in Romans 5:1-5. Notice especially in these verses the phrases, "justified by faith" (a past tense in verse 1), "we have peace" (a present tense in verse 1), and "we have...access to this grace" (a present tense in verse 2):

> Therefore, since we are justified by faith, we have peace with God through our Lord Jesus Christ. Through him we have obtained access to this grace in which we stand, and we rejoice in our hope of sharing

the glory of God. More than that, we rejoice in our sufferings, knowing that suffering produces endurance, and endurance produces character, and character produces hope, and hope does not disappoint us, because God's love has been poured into our hearts through the Holy Spirit which has been given to us.

Finally in this regard, we direct the reader's attention to Romans 1:16-17 also, and the word "salvation."

> For I am not ashamed of the gospel: it is the power of God for salvation to every one who has faith, to the Jew first and also to the Greek. For in it the righteousness of God is revealed through faith for faith; as it is written, "He who through faith is righteous shall live."

In this context, therefore, salvation entails not only justification, but the whole growth process – justification, sanctification, and glorification. The just "shall live" by faith, not simply be justified by faith. So the very life principle of the people of God will be determined by faithfulness to their Creator throughout life, and such faithfulness must inevitably manifest itself in appropriate deeds and actions. Christians have a glorious hope for the future and now partake in a new kind of life.

As we noted earlier in this study, justification is a "once for all" act, in space and time, on the part of God. Due to the universal presence of sin, man would ordinarily be condemned when he appeared before the throne of the holy God, but in view of his faith in Christ, God pronounces the redeemed man "not guilty" by virtue of the finished work of Christ at Calvary. Such justification is ours by obedient faith. Sanctification, however, is a continuous growth process from the initial response to the gospel, through life, culminating in physical death. For this reason, sanctification concerns us now, in the present time, and therefore is a very important and ever contemporary consideration. Once we become new creatures and stand justified in the presence of God, we return to active pursuit of the purpose for which we were originally intended – that purpose being to live a life which manifests love for God with all our heart, mind, soul, and strength. Due to God's love for us, even though we showed ourselves his enemies, we will be moved to trust him and serve him in a devoted attitude of perpetual joy. But what does this love and service toward God really entail? It means that in our present life, we are in a new and living relationship with each of the three personalities of the Godhead. Such a relationship involves some very definite and understandable principles.

The first of these principles is that God, the Creator and Sustainer of life, becomes our Father and we become his adopted children. The apostle John points to this truth when he writes, "to all who received him, who believed in his name, he gave power to become children of God" (John 1:12). God gave sonship to us. It is a gift to be appropriated, not a natural endowment to be taken for granted. The new birth entails the Lord accomplishing for us something far more radical and fundamental than a mere reformation of our character, too. In the new birth, nothing less than the creation of a new being in the place of the old takes place. This newness is so different that a new name and special designation is required – son of God! The natural man can only remain the natural man regardless of how moral he may become. No amount of self-denial, or self-discipline, or self-motivation can make us into even a close resemblance to the kind of character God desires for us. In Christ, however, the natural man can rise on the scale of being to aspire to and achieve new aims, new standards, new likes and dislikes, new possibilities, and even new powers. In short, we are changed into new creatures. Christ gives us the power to become sons of God. Christ lifts us into a nobler lifestyle to the point where we are able to do and be what no one outside Christ can do or hope to be. Sonship means that we are loved, forgiven, and empowered to become like Christ, our image and model. And the more we focus our lives on him, the more we become sons like him. Listen again to John: "Beloved, we are God's children *now*; it does not yet appear what we shall be..." (1 John 3:2).

Once we realize the possibility of this new relationship with God as our Father, we are confronted with the question of how to react to it. The apostle Paul speaks of those who are "holding the form of religion but denying the power of it" (2 Tim. 3:5). This is a description of far too many Christians who go through the practices which are associated with religion but never experience, nor expect to experience, any transforming power in their lives. In contrast to this, the gospel declares that a new and dynamic relationship with God is available to all men. All men are potentially sons of God. In the lives of some, this has become an actuality, but such a reality is not automatic or inevitable. So, some of us may "miss the boat," if we are not careful. There was not a supernatural or magic power which produced such a relationship for them. Rather it was the determination toward dying to self and the consistent focusing of one's life on Christ that produced this new relationship. When we also personally come to terms with these facts, and do this very thing, we, too, can enjoy this blessed new life.

There are so many in our world today who have this potential and so could realize in a personal way what it means to be sons of God. In fact, all have the potential. Yet the truth is that most either decline the opportunity or else they fitfully deny the power of God available to make them sons of God. But here again we emphasize one of Paul's declarations in his informative writings: "Therefore, if *any one* is in Christ, he is a new creation; the old has passed away, behold, the new has come" (2 Cor. 5:17).

The most dangerous idea to ever crop up in the minds of men is the false notion that right form, right doctrine, and right ritual alone constitute the whole of true religion. This philosophy flatly denies the reality of the power of God which constitutes the energizing force which frees up men from the onerous straitjacket of sin and makes them into new creatures – sons of God. In harmony with Paul's words in 2 Timothy 3:5, quoted above, such a religion is only formal and conventional, yet it is without any real life and devoid of the power essential to sustain the believer. True religion is spiritual and external. It is worship from the heart (spiritual), and it expresses itself in public, corporate services, as well as moral behavior (external).

Belonging to God as a son or daughter, on the level of moral and spiritual choice, is a matter for each individual to decide for himself. One must respond by exercising his divinely bestowed manhood, his freedom of choice, his will power. God has made the first and most important move toward man, but man must respond. God has summoned man out of the world, through his Son, and has given him the marvelous opportunity to become something far superior to what he has been. The grace of God has been generously bestowed, and is ever seeking to bring all men into the divine fellowship. But for God to move further, before man responds, would be to violate his nature and the character of his essential personality. Man, therefore, needs heartily and earnestly to pray, "Lord, I believe; help thou mine unbelief" (Mark 9:24, KJV).

Why do so many complain that they do not experience the reality of the fatherhood of God in their lives? The real problem is that these individuals are effectively fleeing from God as the prophet Jonah did in the Old Testament. We more or less separate ourselves from God rather than allow our lifestyles and attitudes to be changed. Here, however, we need to understand something that the Psalmist came to appreciate in the course of his meditations. He stated it in the form of a question: "Whither shall I flee from thy presence?" (Psa. 139:7). In reality, of course, it is impossible to flee from God. There is nowhere on the planet to go where one might not in some way or another find the word of God, faith, the Spirit, or the knowledge of God. Furthermore, God will not allow us to simply go our own way. He persists in seeking us out in the sometimes vain hope that we will come to our senses and cease resisting his overtures. His love drives him to pursue us. He is not wishing that any should perish but that all should come to repentance and embrace his love (cf. 2 Pet. 3:9b). Our God offers us an adoptive sonship on a par with that of his own Son, Jesus. What shall we do with this offer? Such a proposal seems almost beyond denying, but many persist in doing so.

Being in a new and living relationship with God as our spiritual Father involves a second connection also: a partnership with God's Son. In his Galatians epistle, Paul assures the obedient believer that in the justification process he has been baptized "into Christ" (Gal. 3:27). And in the Epistle to the Ephesians, the apostle emphasizes over and over again that once the believer responds to the gospel he has entered a new estate: he is "in Christ." Now when Paul speaks of this union with Christ, as he does in Romans 6:5, he suggests a figure that is not unfamiliar with us or his first century readers – the resurrection! The Christian's hope rests in the fact of the death, burial, and bodily resurrection of Christ. In baptism we are buried in the watery grave and raised up to walk in a new life, or a new relationship with God as Father and with Jesus Christ as elder brother.

In this new and exciting relationship with the Son of God, there is artfully pictured in the Bible the mystical union the Christian enjoys with Jesus Christ. Because of our ready access to Christ as helpful friend, we can rejoice in the hope that we have for sharing in his character and divine nature. We lost this hope due to the persistent presence of sin in our lives, but "in Christ" we can regain this hope.

The risen, ascended, and glorified Son of God is the one that we are to grow toward as our exemplar until we are "made full" and in complete harmony and perfect identity with him: "And we all, with unveiled face, beholding the glory of the Lord, are being changed into his likeness from one degree of glory to another; for this comes from the Lord who is the Spirit" (2 Cor. 3:18). His love is poured into our hearts and when this has occurred it becomes the primary and determining force of our lives. Without this spiritual power we are nothing, but with it we are capable of reaching our spiritual goals, and so we rejoice, for it is the foundational key to our quest for spiritual maturity. From Paul's writings, we determine that such growth will result in the following spiritual realities:

- A love for Christ and a loyalty to him which will motivate us to serve what we perceive to be his purpose for our lives.

- Such a keen awareness of his presence that we live continually in relationship and fellowship with him.

- An attitude of life so receptive to his commands that our heart, mind, and will are continually directed by his Spirit within.

In speaking of Paul's relationship with Christ, James S. Stewart perceptively wrote,

> The heart of Paul's religion is union with Christ....Paul beheld Christ summoning and welcoming him in infinite love into vital unity with Himself. If one seeks for the most characteristic sentences the apostle ever wrote, they will be found...where his intense intimacy with Christ comes to expression. Everything that religion meant for Paul is focused for us in such great words as these: "I live, yet not I, but Christ liveth in me" (Gal. 2:20). "There is, therefore, now no condemnation to them which are in Christ Jesus" (Rom. 8:1). "He that is joined unto the Lord is one spirit" (1 Cor. 6:17).[1]

The relationship, identity, and union which the Christian enjoys with Jesus, is not meant to be a vague or ill-defined kind of relationship. This fact is patently evident from Paul's forceful announcement: "It is no longer I who live, but Christ who lives in me" (Gal. 2:20). This statement must also be seen in connection with Galatians 1:16 where Paul wrote that God "was pleased to reveal his

---

[1] James S. Stewart. *A Man in Christ.* New York: Harper & Bros., pg. 147.

Son *to* [Greek - *in*] me." In certain kinds of mysticism, the personality of the individual is engulfed in an impersonal process and so is ultimately somehow lost in this new reality. Not so in the Christian faith, however. The strong personal quality which is characteristic of the Christian faith not only safeguards all true personal values, but it also strengthens and develops them beyond their previous potential. "In Christ" we will for the first time fully find ourselves. The new life will no longer be like the former one, dependent upon our struggling and frequently frustrated efforts to draw near to God. Rather, Christ himself is the spiritual force within us, as the vine is the source of life to the branches. Christ is the sole meaning of life for the Christian. Every moment is passed in conscious dependence on him. This is the new life, and it is intensely personal. It is, in its essence, faith in and union with Christ who loved us and gave himself for us.

The new personal life we are offered "in Christ" is given cogency and resiliency by being further described in other passages in the New Testament. Jesus speaks of this new life to the Jewish elder statesman and Sanhedrin council member Nicodemus in John 3:1-15. It is the regenerative action of the Spirit of Christ which translates and transforms us into new creatures, pulls us back from the edge, and invests us with a new life close to God and his Son. Life in Christ bestows upon us the glorious liberty of God's children and we are no longer the wretched prisoners of this world. In spite of the fact that, as ordinary men caught up in the lusts and pleasures of this confusing world, we have fallen away from a relationship with Christ due to sin, "the righteousness of God has been manifested" (Rom. 3:21) by his offer of justification through obedient faith in Christ. This has an amazing impact upon our psychology, and it means that no one, the aged or the youthful, the sick or the healthy, the bright or the dull, need to be living a humdrum, defeated existence. Due to one's relationship with Jesus the Son, human lives can be and are quite often radically changed. A faith directed toward the Son of God will assure the believer enjoyment of the status of sonship with God due to our acceptance of the redemptive work of Christ. And this, in turn, will bring to the believer a heightened quality of spirituality. It is the relationship of union with Christ that brings growth toward spiritual maturity in the life lived in the contemporary world. In spite of its mundane and prosaic character in a variety of ways, there remains the fact that, "It is no longer I who live, but Christ who lives in me; and the life I now live in the flesh I live by faith in the Son of God" (Gal. 2:20). It is Christ who makes our lives special, even extraordinary!

As we have seen, one thing leads to another just as the night follows the day: being in a new and living relationship with God as Father involves a new and living relationship with Jesus the Son. Now these two relationships also involve a third and equally valuable association – one with the Holy Spirit as Counselor. When an individual is declared justified in Christ, having met God's simple terms for justification, he is immediately indwelt by the Holy Spirit. This Spirit is portrayed as having the redeeming power of God to penetrate profoundly into the old life as a new dynamic and a renewing strength. Thus, through obedient faith, the believer is intimately united with the Father, the Son, and the Holy Spirit. It is through this magnificent union that the individual becomes a new being and enters into that new relationship where he or she shares in the life of God. As the Holy Spirit was the motivating power in the birth, life, and resurrection of our Lord, so he is the empowering gift which makes it possible for the faithful to be born anew and resurrected to a new way of life, free from the compulsion to persist in the commission of sin. The work of the Spirit is to transform the believer gradually over time and through experience into the image of Christ (cf. 2 Cor. 3:18).

The apostle Peter made the following promise to the multitude that assembled to hear him preach in Jerusalem on the day of Pentecost: "Repent, and be baptized every one of you in the name of Jesus Christ for the forgiveness of your sins; and you shall receive the gift of the Holy Spirit" (Acts 2:38). Now when Peter set forth this spiritual contract, he was doing nothing more than repeating the pledge made earlier by Christ to him and his fellow disciples: "I will pray the Father, and he will give you another Counselor, to be with you for ever, even the Spirit of truth, whom the world cannot receive, because it neither sees him nor knows him; you know him, for he dwells with you, and will be in you" (John 14:16-17). The essence of this prediction was that the Holy Spirit would work effectively within the disciples of Christ to support and guide them in the ongoing work they had been commissioned to do in the world. This Spirit would tellingly transform and effectually energize the small band of defeated disciples. He would be the motivating power of a new quality of life – life lived in the Spirit. And the ministry of the Spirit would be a continuation of the life and teaching of Jesus (cf. John 15:26; 16:13). The departure of their Lord from their physical presence into heaven did not mean that the disciples were left unsupported and unguided. On the contrary, the Spirit of Christ would remain with them forever: "In that day you will know that I am in my Father and you in me, and I in you" (John 14:20). To be joined with the Spirit of Christ and to have the Spirit of Christ present with us is not just a gift reserved for us after our earthly life is finished. For, as Paul puts it, whether we live or die, we are with the Lord and he is with us (cf. Rom. 14:8).

Jesus also makes it plain that what he has promised to his apostles will be available not only to the disciples present at that time, but also to all who have his commandments and keep them (cf. John 14:21). The whole tone and tenor of Jesus' remarks concerning the coming Counselor imply permanency and continual presence. The conclusion which we are led to draw from this, then, is that the individual who follows after Jesus and who strives to do his will shall not be alone in his continuing quest toward eternal life. He will not be orphaned, or in the desperate struggles in which faith is sometimes intrinsically involved. Rather, he enjoys an ongoing presence in his life that gives comfort and grants him the knowledge that he is never "all by himself." As the Lord said, "If a man loves me, he will keep my word, and my Father will love him, and we will come to him and make our home with him" (John 14:23).

The apostle Paul also speaks elsewhere regarding the fact of the indwelling Spirit of Christ. In his meditations, he recognizes that the success of the Christian in living that quality of life our Lord set forth for him is continuously dependent upon the inner dynamic of the Holy Spirit as a living partner in our efforts. He further assures us that such a quality of life is possible for us because we do not any longer truly belong to the natural order of the world: "You are not in the flesh, you are in the Spirit, if in fact the Spirit of God dwells in you. Any one who does not have the Spirit of Christ does not belong to him" (Rom. 8:9). A few theorists have attempted to argue that Paul has, by a nebulous process of unaided human reflection, or by an unproven ideological borrowing from pagan philosophies, arrived at the theory that Christians are endowed with a mystical power which he chooses to call the Holy Spirit.[2] The apostle, however, is not concerned with a doctrine, or a philosophy, but a wholesome fact of spiritual existence. He realizes the undeniable persistent presence of a higher power in his life that makes it possible for him to face difficult situations, to receive and realize truths of God, and to live a lifestyle that before he thought impossible for him to live. He knows, too, that this higher power is the Holy Spirit, which comes to the Christian as a lasting possession upon obedience to God in Christ. There is in his language the realization of a dependable permanence and an authentic intimacy in this relationship also which the Christian shares with the Holy Spirit, and which transcends description by mere words. Faithful obedience is the key which unlocks, for the believer, this great source of energy and fellowship. Such a yielding humility is a human response which brings us to a source of divine power which can work in and with us to help us realize victory in Christ.

We recognize here again the weakness of the works-salvation tendency which we as self-conscious human beings ever face. We always confront the temptation to depend on certain forms of belief and the right kind of orthodoxy to make us spiritual. Or again, we prefer a particular standard of good works to insure that we gain that victorious life in Christ. Yet we soon discover that right form, right doctrine, and right ritual, without the power of the Spirit of Christ in our lives, is ultimately defeating. The law, as strong as it is, can never lead us to realize victorious spiritual living because it is by its very nature "weak through the flesh." What the Christian needs is a new energy, a more potent quality of life. Man cannot rightfully serve God, no matter how plain his will is and no matter how strong his own will is to do so. Man is bent on the things of the world and has no natural inclination toward or intrinsic capacity for the higher things of God. His mind must be changed from a carnal into a spiritual mind. This process of changing is the product of the work of the Holy Spirit within. The power that animates the Christian is the Spirit of Christ dwelling within. It is this Spirit within that enables man to withstand all the hostile forces allied against him and to at-

---

[2] Paul clearly parts company here with pagan philosophers, however, because the individual Christian never becomes a mere instrument of the Spirit. The believer in Christ remains a person, and a person can never be used as a mere tool.

tain that Christ-like life which seems unattainable and always in his own strength beyond his reach. For Paul, the power that God gives to all Christians – the Holy Spirit within – is that intense power which is changing the Christian's nature into the nature of Christ. As this Spirit raised our Lord mightily from the dead, he raises us also if we are faithful into a new life which is no longer like that of the natural man we used to be.

On two more occasions, Paul mentions the fact that the Christian is indwelt by the Holy Spirit. When writing to the church at Corinth, he says, "Do you not know that you are God's temple and that God's Spirit dwells in you?" (1 Cor. 3:16) and "Do you not know that your body is a temple of the Holy Spirit within you, which you have from God?" (1 Cor. 6:19). We are not alone! The inner presence of the Holy Spirit is the spiritual birthright of every Christian. The Spirit is not a natural possession of all men, but has come through the command of the resurrected Christ to all obedient believers. When this Spirit is permitted to enter in and infuse all of our activities, changes will begin to take place within our lives. The presence and activity of this heavenly gift assures us that God is not a remote Being enthroned on high but is genuinely near to us and highly effective in our lives. He dwells in our hearts and energizes and inspires our inner being to the extent that he will quite readily and obviously be seen in the ethical qualities of our lives. It is because of this that Christ becomes a vital and personal force in the life of the Christian. In fact, Paul speaks of "the Spirit of Christ" (Rom. 8:9) and "the Spirit of life in Christ Jesus" (Rom. 8:2), and brings it all together by saying, "the Lord is the Spirit" (2 Cor. 3:17). To know Christ is to be in Christ and to be in Christ is to have the Spirit of Christ. The result of this is to have lives ruled by this Spirit and to have life eternal even in the context of an otherwise thoroughly physical existence. "To set the mind on the Spirit is life and peace" (Rom. 8:6).

So, as a result of the believer's acceptance of Christ as Savior personal sin and guilt are removed and fellowship is established with God as Father, Christ as Brother, and the Holy Spirit as Counselor. In Christ the believer is in a relationship with the entire Trinity. The result is that the personal life of a Christian is a matter of intimate and personal relationships with God, Christ, and the Holy Spirit. There is always the very human tendency to forget this, however, and view the Christian faith in impersonal terms, to view it rather as a system of doctrines, or as a mere code of ethics. But the good news is that God has made himself personally known as Father, Son, and Holy Spirit. The Christian faith asserts that to be in the body of Christ is not simply a matter of embracing proper beliefs or conducting one's life in conformity with certain ethical standards, but a personal relationship of mutual love and concern. The end result of all this is that now, *today*, the Christian stands justified and in a personal relationship with the Godhead – the Father, The Son, and the Holy Spirit. This is not simply a doctrinal statement, either, but a reality that we can and should experience now!

At the beginning of this chapter, we addressed ourselves to the fact of justification. We pointed out that it is a "once for all time" work of God on behalf of the Christian, performed at the cross of Christ. Sanctification, on the other hand, is a moment by moment way of life – a daily walk with involves personal growth in intimacy or fellowship with God, Christ, and the Holy Spirit. Sanctification is living in harmony with God's will for us each day, or to put it another way, living a life of love for God and neighbor. John characterizes it in the following words: "For this is the love of God, that we keep his commandments. And his commandments are not burdensome" (1 John 5:3). The new life in Christ gives the Christian an otherworldly nature. Because the believer shares in God's nature, he is endowed with God's, or the Spirit's heavenly life, which energizes him with the power to obey. In his second epistle to Corinth, Paul writes, "God is able to provide you with every blessing in abundance, so that you may always have enough of everything and may provide in abundance for every good work" (2 Cor. 9:8). By ourselves we can do nothing. In our unredeemed state we are in hopeless bondage to self and subject to the evils of this natural world. But being conscious of the inward presence of the Spirit of Christ, we have the strength to overcome the world. Whatever the circumstances by which we are led into our obedience to the will of God, we can be confident that the indwelling Spirit will enable us to do all that needs to be done in that situation and in those circumstances. The Spirit within assures us that we will have the strength to align ourselves with the will of God so that "his commandments are not burdensome" (1 John 5:3; cf. Phil. 4:13; Eph. 3:16-17).

Perhaps we ought to peer below the surface, however, and in-quire, "Are his commandments actually burdensome?" The truth of the matter is that many of us do find the commandments of our Lord to be downright onerous. In point of fact, there are times when we can hardly find many of them bearable. What does this mean? Does it signify that I am wrong, or that I must work harder, or that I do not have the Holy Spirit within? It cannot mean that I have not been justified, for justification is the work of God on my behalf and it stands firm for as long as I am in Christ. It cannot mean that I do not have the Spirit within, for we have already seen that this is a prom-ise granted to all baptized believers. What does it mean then? Let us read and reflect upon John's words again: "For this is the love of God, that we keep his commandments. And his commandments are not burdensome. For whatever is born of God overcomes the world; and *this is the victory* that overcomes the world, *our faith*" (1 John 5:3-4). What is the victory that overcomes the world? Our faith!

The central problem in our life is how to overcome the things of the world that would lure us away from God. The man Jesus Christ, the incarnate Son of God, has already done this for us, however. He has overcome sin on our behalf (2 Cor. 5:21)! The spiritual victory has already been courageously won and definitively completed for us on the basis of the finished work of Christ.[3] What a daring claim this is! Victory belongs not to the world and the forces of evil which surround us, in spite of our daily struggles, but to the crucified Christ and those who believe in him. Our obedience and acceptance of Christ as Savior and Lord make this victory our own. We have over-come the world and so we share in the victory, and we can keep on conquering with the help and power of the Spirit of Christ within. We must believe this, no matter how much our traditional Western philosophy of work ethics inwardly rebels against the idea. It is the world and its considerable power which makes the commandments appear to us on the surface of things to be onerous. The new birth, however, gives us a new otherworldly nature and a strength which overcomes the world. If we try to live the Christian life and keep the

---

[3] In 1 John 5:4, the apostle says, "This is the victory which overcomes the world." The phrase, "which overcomes" (*hē nikēsasa*), is aorist tense – which in the Greek expresses a single act in the past, not continued or repeated.

commandments of our Lord in our own strength alone (and many of us may be striving to do just this), we will still be burdened by the commandments. But if we live moment by moment under the realization, or *faith*, that in Christ the victory has already been won for us, we will more readily and joyfully serve the Lord. The new life imparted to believers motivates us not only with the desire to do God's will, but it also empowers us to give effect to that desire. The way for the Lord's commands to become less burdensome for us is to recognize the victory won for us by the crucified and resurrected Lord, and then utilize the power given us through the agency of the indwelling Holy Spirit. We must live in this faith moment by moment, for to do so is victory.

Thus, the victory we have is faith – faith centered in Jesus Christ and God's action in his incarnation and vicarious suffering on our behalf. This faith is no mere vague belief that accepts the appearance of the historical Jesus and the bare facts of his life, death, and resurrection alone, but a faith that believes that he truly did overcome the world and infuses us with the confidence that we can share in his victory. This is exactly what our Lord urges us to believe: "In the world you have tribulation; be of good cheer, I have overcome the world" (John 16:33). In Christ we share in this grand triumph. By our faith in Jesus as the Son of God we are so united with him that his victory becomes our own. We conquer by his power. As we were buried and raised with him in the waters of baptism, so we are raised to a new life of spiritual triumph. "Little children, you are of God, and have overcome...for he who is in you is greater than he who is in the world" (1 John 4:4).

The Christian life, therefore, is not a meaningless tragic drama of repeated failures. It is, rather, a glorious fellowship with God, Christ, and the Holy Spirit. The commandments of God are not slavish drudgery either, but an opportunity for us to make of ourselves co-laborers with the Godhead toward the perfecting of our souls, suiting them for heaven. Christ came in the flesh and won the victory over the flesh for us. Faith in him and his victory over sin and death releases the power of God for us as we face the struggles in day-to-day living. Do we fervently believe this and genuinely benefit by it? Do we believe that "in everything God works for good with those who love him" (Rom. 8:28)? If so then we can say with Paul, "thanks be to God, who gives us the victory through our Lord Jesus Christ" (1 Cor. 15:57).

Discussion Questions

1. How would you respond to one whose view of God is as a gracious grandfatherly-type who easily forgives sins? _____

_____

_____

_____

2. Define the difference between justification and sanctification as it applies to one's life. _____

_____

3. What are the implications and differences between a "natural" moral individual and a moral individual "in Christ"? _____

_____

_____

_____

4. According to the apostle Paul (cf. 2 Cor. 3:18), what is the function of the Holy Spirit in our personal lives? _____

_____

_____

_____

X. The Christian's Responsibility – Fruitfulness

In summary, in the last chapter we observed that when an individual accepts Christ as Savior, sin and guilt are removed, and communication and fellowship are established with God as Father, Christ as Brother, and the Holy Spirit as Counselor. The Christian is now very much a part in a permanent family setting; he is in Christ and in fellowship with the Godhead. The resulting fellowship is meant to be one that is intimate and personal. And with this relationship also come all the attendant spiritual blessings of God – forgiveness, justification, sanctification, glorification, and life eternal. But it is the divine intention that there is also to be a state of spiritual fruitfulness which characterizes our lives generally. The natural result of fellowship with God is that the one who has entered into and remains in this association will demonstrate in many and varied ways a determination toward spiritual fruitfulness. The power of the living Christ will necessarily produce changes within us. This divine prerogative within us ought naturally to produce fruitfulness, as the apostle Paul assures us: "My brethren, you have died to the law through the body of Christ, so that you may belong to another, to him who has been raised from the dead in order that *we may bear fruit* for God" (Rom. 7:4). Notice these two very simple but extraordinarily profound statements: (1) we belong to Christ, and (2) we bear fruit. The union with Christ means that we live lives acceptable to God and useful for his purposes. Nowhere in God's word is there any teaching which leads us to believe that a Christian can be passive and non-fruitful and still be acceptable under the biblical definition of what a "Christian" is intended to be. In the words of the Psalmist, the child of God is to be "like a tree planted by streams of water" (Psa. 1:3), and so have all the necessary nourishment available from God to develop and bear spiritual fruit. If our fellowship with the Godhead does not sharpen and intensify our perception of the need for fruit-bearing, then we must question either the clarity of our understanding of such things or else the reality of this fellowship.

With these thoughts in mind, we realize that the test which we are to apply to ourselves in relation to our fellowship with God in this particular situation is objective rather than subjective. The Holy Spirit, who bears witness to our fellowship with the Godhead in the scriptures, completes his testimony in our individual characters. If we are in fellowship with God, this fellowship will not be very long in bringing about a change in our manner of life. Always and forever, the Christian life in fellowship with God is to be tested by the nature of its various fruits. We are confronted daily with some very real and objective opportunities for demonstration of these verities. As well, there are some questions we need to ask in such situations. A few of them are as follows: (a) Have I become more outgoing and less self-involved? (b) Am I more thoughtful of others? (c) Am I more willing to accept blame for those things that are my fault and less willing to criticize? (d) Am I more disciplined and less self-indulgent? (e) Has my horizon grown and have my concrete concerns expanded from self and loved ones to neighbors and community, to the nation and the world? (f) Do I accept responsibility and get things accomplished, or do I find fault and make excuses to cover my inaction? From these questions, and our attempts at responding to them as regards our personal life, we are made keenly aware that our fellowship with God is not real unless it produces within our lives a self-giving, or better yet, a Christ-like way of life in the world in which we live. Our lives must be purged of self-indulgent egoism and brought to a state of more advanced spiritual maturity. Our Lord put it in this manner:

> If any man would come after me, let him deny himself and take up his cross daily and follow me (Luke 9:23), [and] A new commandment I give to you, that you love one another; even as I have loved you, that you also love one another. By this all men will know that you are my disciples, if you have love for one another (John 13:34-35).

In relation to fruit-bearing, the apostle Paul issues a very sober warning to the Roman brethren: "Do not yield your members to sin as instruments of wickedness, but yield yourselves to God as men who have been brought from death to life, and your members to God as instruments of righteousness" (Rom. 6:13). In Christ, the apostle says that we must consider ourselves "dead to sin and alive to God in Christ Jesus" (Rom. 6:11). From this, Paul draws a number of necessary practical deductions, and such deductions entail the necessity of working out in our ordinary daily lives the moral results of being alive to God and dead to the world. In his Phillippian epistle, Paul urges his brethren to be "filled with the fruits of righteousness which come through Jesus Christ" (Phil. 1:11). It is not enough to be doctrinally sound and pure, even though these are not matters of insignificance in their own right. Our lives must reveal our relationship with God in the presence and prevalence of righteous and noble activity. Our faith response to right doctrine must be met equally by a conduct response in our daily life that is entirely consistent and completely in harmony with that faith. Our fellowship with the Godhead must manifest itself in righteous deeds. And notice again, according to Paul in Philippians 1:11, such fruit comes "through Jesus Christ." Fruit-bearing is not something about which we can boast, however; rather it is the blessed gift of God dynamically working in us due to our faith and trust.

We cannot, therefore, divorce the spiritual truths which we have been emphasizing throughout this book from the practical applications to what we know to be the true will of God for our lives. Paul would have been the last man on earth to permit right doctrine to be separated from practical day-to-day responsibilities in the community of faithful men. Our responsibilities in the practical area of fruit-bearing cannot be lost in an empty and passive response to right doctrine and proper worship. In Christ we have a new mind and are being transformed into a new person. The Spirit of Christ is working to fashion and frame our total life by enduring principles of righteousness. And it is the Holy Spirit who gives us this power for righteousness, peace, and newness of life. This is the power about which Paul speaks when he writes these words:

> For sin will have no dominion over you, since you are not under law but under grace. What then? Are we to sin because we are not under law but under grace? By no means! Do you not know that if you yield yourselves to any one as obedient slaves, you are slaves of the one whom you obey, either of sin, which leads to death, or of obedience, which leads to righteousness? But thanks be to God, that you who

were once slaves of sin have become obedient from the heart to the standard of teaching to which you were committed, and, having been set free from sin, have become slaves of righteousness. I am speaking in human terms, because of your natural limitations. For just as you once yielded your members to impurity and to greater and greater iniquity, so now yield your members to righteousness for sanctification (Rom. 6:14-19).

Too many Christians, however, manifest persistent weakness rather than spiritual strength, in their lives. We need to be disturbed and awakened to the true state of things concerning this perpetual problem, especially in view of the power that is made available to us when God is permitted to take control of our lives. In Christ we are given the ability to distinguish between right and wrong, and the power to live a righteous and courageous life. To remain passive and ineffective when God has given us all that we have, and has made so much more accessible to us, is to betray our Lord. We have the indwelling Spirit to enlighten, strengthen, and produce fruitful lives. We have the word, the power of God for salvation (Rom. 1:16). We have the fellowship of believers to sustain and encourage us on an ongoing basis. To remain spiritually weak is to deny the reality and efficacy of all the power that has been made available to us in Christ.

What do we say to all of this? Reflection on such matters makes us aware that, in spite of our comprehension of the new life in Christ, in spite of our knowledge of the spiritual reality and powers from our Lord, and in spite of our justification and development in sanctification, it is still possible for us to bring forth the fruit of the world instead of the fruit of the Spirit. How is this possible? It is possible because we still have alternative options available to us, and so we can yield ourselves to that old master we served prior to our commitment of ourselves to Christ. This very real danger was pointed out by Jesus in his insightful parable of the evil spirits:

When the unclean spirit has gone out of a man, he passes through waterless places seeking rest, but he finds none. Then he says, "I will return to my house from which I came." And when he comes he finds it empty, swept, and put in order. Then he goes and brings with him seven other spirits more evil than himself, and they enter and dwell there; and the last state of that man becomes worse than the first. So shall it be also with this evil generation (Matt. 12:43-45).

It is within the realm of the possible for us to recognize that we have passed from death to life and yet continue to allow sin to manifest its presence and reassert its power in our lives. If we persistently neglect the use of the spiritual powers we have in Christ and stubbornly fail to grow spiritually with the opportunities given us by God, eventually moral weakness will set in. God re-created us in his Son as an abode for the Spirit's indwelling and an avenue for his considerable power. Our life becomes dead again if and when we fail to utilize this indwelling power in cultivating the fruits of the Spirit. This reveals again the undeniable principle that Christian living entails more than just passive reflection upon proper things and exercising ourselves with right ritual. It requires a dying to self and the world and then allowing the Spirit of Christ to fill the resulting void left in our lives. Jesus is the way, the path by which we are to walk; he is the truth, the light to guide our walk; he is the life, the power to sustain us in our walk. Such power, if it is allowed to have its way in us, will enable us to say with Paul, "I can do all things in him who strengthens me" (Phil. 4:13).

When we enter into a determined relationship with the Godhead and receive the gracious gift of the Holy Spirit, the Spirit takes up residence within us as the agent of the complete Trinity. All obedient believers possess or receive this Spirit and hence share in the life of God. The results of such a marvelous and blessed spiritual relationship and the consequent indwelling power which grows out of it will soon be evident in our lives: "The fruit of the Sprit is love, joy, peace, patience, kindness, goodness, faithfulness, gentleness, self-control..." (Gal. 5:22-23). The Spirit thus serves to distinguish the believer from all non-believers. The evidence of spiritual renewal lies in the fact that Christians live in a way possible only for those who have experienced regeneration.

In spite of all this, there remains that other possibility that we have discussed and must always be aware of, however. We must know that God is ever the perfect gentleman, a polite guest in our home who will not force himself upon us, nor will he insist when we are unwilling to do so, that we listen to him or conform ourselves to his will. Just as clearly evident in the Scriptures is the ugly possibility for our lives to produce the sordid fruits of the world; our heavenly guest will stand aside while we waste all of our gifts and squander his mercies: "The works of the flesh are plain: fornication, impurity, licentiousness, idolatry, sorcery, enmity, strife, jealousy, anger, selfishness, dissension, party spirit, envy, drunkenness, carousing, and the like" (Gal. 5:19-21). We emphasize again that it is entirely within the realm of the possible for us to yield ourselves to the wrong power and bring forth the fruit of the world. By so doing, we can actually bar ourselves from the kingdom of God. We reveal to the world that we are without the regenerating power of faith. We are guilty of prostituting the power of God for a less noble way of life. To illustrate this, consider the case of a black married couple. After a normal delivery, it is discovered that the wife has given birth to a white child. All of the world would know immediately that this woman had been unfaithful to her husband. In a similar fashion, it is altogether possible for Christians to do the unlikely thing, the unnatural thing, the unseemly and abhorrent thing – and bring forth the fruit of the world and thus unfortunately fail to bear the expected fruit of the Spirit. Such a situation would constitute flagrant spiritual unfaithfulness, or spiritual adultery, on our part.

When we think very long on this concept, we recognize that the word "faith" has a much deeper and more significant meaning than we have often tended to attribute to it. As faith is the essential instrument by which we gain victory (cf. 1 John 5:3-4), it is also the necessary instrument by which we bear the proper fruit. The reality of our faith and of our new life in Christ is revealed by our break with the darkness of the natural world and its abominable fruits. In the words of Paul, "Those who belong to Christ Jesus have crucified the flesh with its passions and desires" (Gal. 5:24). And notice again what we saw so clearly before, namely that our victory is the result of belonging to Jesus Christ. We are just as incapable of crucifying the flesh and its passions and desires in our own strength alone as we are of saving ourselves. We are made fruitful "by God's power" (1 Pet. 1:5). This should be a source of both confidence and joy for every child of God.

We are indwelt by the Holy Spirit of God to the intent and for the purpose of being a usable agent, empowered to bring forth the fruit of the Spirit. This being true, we must consider the nature of our response to the Spirit in our lives. Paul writes, "If we live by the Spirit, let us also walk by the Spirit" (Gal. 5:25). From this scripture we recognize that we have a part to play in the Spirit's operation in our lives. God has not made us automatons incapable of responding either one way or the other. We are fully autonomous, and so we must allow our lives to be shaped and molded by the will and mind of the Spirit of Christ. There must be conformity between our outward way of life and the inner Spirit. This is important, for to be directed by the Spirit results in the inevitable presence of the fruit of the Spirit and in our living for the higher things of the Spirit. If the Spirit is to be the source of our life, then we must allow the Spirit freely to direct our course.

As we reflect further on what it means to allow the Spirit to direct our course in life, we are made keenly aware of several warnings given in the scriptures which deal with our relationship with the Spirit. The first of these warnings is from Paul's letter to the Ephesians: "Do not grieve the Holy Spirit of God, in whom you were sealed for the day of redemption" (Eph. 4:30). The Spirit of God does not exercise dominion over us to the extent that we have no control over ourselves. We are not without either the will or the strength to resist his desires for us. He seeks a voluntary submission so that his will can dominate in the believer's life for our ultimate good. The Spirit does exercise restraint in our lives in that he keeps us secure in Christ and empowers us for the work of God. The Spirit does this, however, in the fullest possible cooperation with us. The ability to produce the fruit of the Spirit in the lives of individual Christians is directly related to the believer's degree of surrender to the will of the divine Spirit within. Therefore, it is possible for the individual Christian to hinder this control of the Spirit, to frustrate his purposes in his life and, thus, grieve the Holy Spirit of God. The degree of control the Spirit has in our lives is dependent on the degree of our own surrender. This means that the control of the Spirit in the life of the Christian varies. The more dedicated individuals will yield more to God's will and thus grieve the Lord less, and in the end prove to be more fruitful. And the truth of the matter is, to be disloyal or unfruitful is not a mere act of disobedience to God's will, not a simple insubordinate deed. It is rather a personal affront to God's Holy Spirit. The Holy Spirit claims us as his sphere of influence, and he is severely wronged by rival claims to our loyalty. The way to avoid this is for us to identify ourselves more fully with the Spirit and his heavenly concerns, rather than identify the Spirit with ourselves and our own often earthly ones. The Spirit's action in us is to be our identity and the world will see in us the resulting fruits of the Spirit.

In speaking to the Jews in Jerusalem, Stephen lashed out against them for their stubborn and persistent refusal to accept Jesus as God's Son: "You stiff-necked people, uncircumcised in heart and ears, you always resist the Holy Spirit" (Acts 7:51). Precisely as did these Jews, it is possible that we, too, can become so unresponsive to the power of the Spirit within our lives that we close our ears to God's words of wisdom for our own well-being and in the end fail to enjoy the benefits of the grace of God. We can so pride ourselves in the outward observance of ritual, even the very covenant sign of baptism and a rigid pattern of what we consider to be right beliefs to the extent and degree that we actually resist the Holy Spirit. Living in such a manner can rob us of spirituality to the extent that we wither away within and bear no fruit to perfection. To resist the Spirit is to lose our capability to perceive the presence and power of God in our life. Faith in Christ, right regard for the scriptures, and a life of service and worship can prove to be quite lifeless and ineffective if divorced from the sovereign and dynamic activity of the Spirit. On the other hand, by being aware of and not resisting the Spirit's influence, we can authenticate our regeneration and make more effective our sanctification.

Because God desires so fervently to work in us by the Spirit, there is a third warning posted on the pages of Scripture, this one being against the possibility of quenching the Spirit: "Do not quench the Spirit," warns Paul (1 Thess. 5:19). On the basis of the finished work of Christ and our obedience to him, it is God's purpose and goal that the fruits of the Spirit should be evident in the lives of Christians. It is possible, however, for the believer to fail to use the power of the Spirit and, thus, by his benign neglect, quench the Spirit. In Thessalonica, Paul saw some of his brethren in a state of idleness, a few of them guilty of immorality and of other sins. Seeing the fruit of the world in their lives, the apostle concluded on the basis of what he observed in them that they were quenching the Spirit. The Spirit would enable them to overcome evil and to produce the fruit of the Spirit, yet the Thessalonians manifested an almost total absence of such spiritual power and of the joy which springs from it. They were, as many are today, failing to recognize and use God's rich provision and gracious concern for us in his gift of the Holy Spirit. Or, perhaps we ought to say that we are failing to allow the Holy Spirit to use us for God's glory.

Failure to work in full cooperation with the Spirit in our personal renewal is serious business indeed. It involves, as it were, controversy with God, stultification of our spiritual life and service, and a repression of the good which lies dormant within us. We can, as we have seen, grieve, resist, and quench the Spirit. We do all of this when we fail to bring forth the necessary fruit of the Spirit. We know, too, that we can be and are urged to be "filled with the Spirit" (Eph. 5:18) and even to be "aglow with the Spirit" (Rom. 12:11). The Christian has not just been given a fresh start and then left to work it out with a modicum of divine assistance. He has been given a new life, and his commission is to live this life in the strength of the Holy Spirit. Because Christ has won the way to victory for believers, and because God has adopted us as his children and given us the Spirit to guarantee our growth toward perfection, it must be to the heart and mind of divinity the deepest kind of sin for us not to allow the Spirit to work in our lives and exhibit the fruits of this relationship. When the believer is not giving absolute permission for this work within, a work made possible by the sacrifice of God's only Son, when this work is not flowing forth in good deeds and spiritual living, then that individual must be unfaithful in the deepest and darkest sense (even though it may never seem so). Our Lord informs us that he has provided for us a way of victory – our faith (cf. 1 John 5:3-4). Christ opened the way for us to be "changed into his likeness from one degree of glory to another" (2 Cor. 3:18). The work of the Spirit within is given in order to illumine our mind, engender faith in our heart, and sanctify us wholly to God as Jesus was. Yet when we grieve, quench, or resist his indwelling power to work this much needed change in us, surely we are guilty of the grossest form of unfaithfulness, of not believing in God and what he says about giving us victory through faith. When we leave the power of the Spirit outside of our life, standing outside with our heart's door closed, we must come to understand that we inadvertently leave also the victory promised to us somewhere out there just beyond our reach.

Realizing the power and potential we have in Christ, some of us are confronted with the fact that we may not be the creative and life-giving force in the world that we know that we should be. This leads us to ask ourselves, "Why are we not bringing forth the fruit of the Spirit as we should? Why do we find that we are always fighting to lift ourselves out of the depths of spiritual and moral atrophy?" In many of our lives this may be due to genuine spiritual ignorance in that we may never have been taught the true meaning and results of the work of Christ in our lives. We have been taught how to become a child of God, but maybe not taught the present-life practical meaning of the work of Christ within each of us. Therefore, many are firmly convinced that once they become Christians, from that point on they must live the Christian life by their own strength and by it alone. Still others do not effectively produce the fruit of the Spirit because they have developed through erroneous instruction a sort of Christian libertinism, that is, the attitude which urges us to "eat, drink, and make merry, for Christ has already accomplished for us all that is necessary to be done." All of these frustration avenues, however, are really only dead-end streets that lead us no where. Legalism, works-salvation, and libertinism, as we have previously seen, are not the paths that lead to spirituality and fruitful lives, even though each of them pretends to be. Rather, the road to spirituality and fruitful living is the road that allows the Spirit of God the freedom to work conspicuously and triumphantly in our lives. When we learn this, when we come to realize fully the meaning of the work of God, Christ and the Holy Spirit in our lives, then a new door to spirituality and creative living will spontaneously be opened to us. When we begin to act on this knowledge, then we will experience a sense of newness as fresh and real as was our initial conversion to Christ. So what is desperately needed in our hearts and heads is the knowledge of the meaning of the work of the Godhead in our lives, coupled with a faith response on our part to that knowledge. This is the genius of Christianity – we have been given the power and capacity for being abundantly renewed and radically restored to a state of spiritual wholeness!

It is however also possible for us to have a knowledge and mental understanding of the work of Christ on our behalf and an appreciation of the power of God's Spirit within, yet never really appropriate this knowledge and understanding in any practical way in our lives. There is always such a danger that we may become preoccupied with various religious forms and typical protocols and petty phrases which in reality extend no further than being an outward expression of an empty husk of true faith, a mere religion of externals. As has been stated before, however, the important thing in the Christian faith is practically to apply and put into practice what we know to be the truth. There are many among the number of those who deem themselves faithful to Christ who understand only shallowly what the Lord desires of them in relation to becoming a disciple and living the Christian life, yet in practical terms they do not apply this understanding in their everyday lives. By stubbornly refusing, or benignly neglecting to follow through on their knowledge, these individuals lose the sharp edge of their conscience and grow dull over time until gradually the power of God at work within their lives becomes a silent voice, muffled by their own lack of a deep resolve. Unfortunately this same principle is equally true in relation to our life of bearing fruit for the Lord. We may know the truth, we may have knowledge and understanding of it necessary for us to embrace it at first, yet we may fail to appropriate these things practically in our lives. The result of this failure ultimately is that we do not bear fruit and we do not grow and develop spiritually.

There are many individuals who would like to grow spiritually and develop into fruit-bearers for the Lord, but they will not put forth the required faith, trust, and effort to produce such a crop. Likewise, the farmer who fails to plow the ground, plant his field, nourish the seedlings with fertilizer, and then wait patiently for the produce which time and a little rain will provide, will be disappointed at harvest season. We often encounter individuals who manifest such spiritual qualities of character and we hear from them their vague longings for spiritual resources which only spiritually mature Christians possess. Sometimes we ourselves, in an hour of stress or trouble, may cry out for spiritual strength and long for growth. Then, when no obvious resource is forthcoming and nothing much seems to happen in response to our "fervent prayer," we conclude that all this talk of the indwelling Spirit and of God's power to re-create us is just so much talk, nothing more than empty theological jargon. It never seems to enter our minds that God's power to work within our lives is dependent not only upon the generosity and efficacy of the divine giver, but to some degree also upon the ready response of the human receiver. As Jesus explained, "Blessed are those who hunger and thirst for righteousness, for they shall be satisfied" (Matt. 5:6).

One of the problems we face at times in our quest for spirituality is that many of us have the desire to be spiritual, but we are satisfied with mediocrity on our own part. We are actually quite satisfied with being well below average in our spirituality, only average in our faithfulness, and just barely average in our personal fruitfulness. The problem is that we do not seek that high goal of advanced spiritual development that comes to us as a gift of God. And how do we attain this very desirable goal? This is where our problem lies. We must hunger and thirst for it.

Now we must realize here that we cannot achieve such spirituality and fruitfulness only by our own personal strength, wisdom, and power. We must be aware of our deep need – we must hunger and thirst. This is no a passing feeling either, or something we experience only in an hour of deep need or haunting stress, but an ever-present awareness of our intrinsic deficiency. Too often we possess this desire like Israel did in the Old Testament. Her desire for true spirituality was often like a "morning cloud," here one minute and gone the next. In contrast, hungering and thirsting are deep and profound needs and even at times painful hurts. Such longing for divine acceptance is expressed very well by the Psalmist in the following lines: "As a [deer] longs for flowing streams, so longs my soul for thee, O God. My soul thirsts for God, for the living God" (Psa. 42:1-2). Blessed is the Christian who is not satisfied with partial or underdeveloped spirituality but is satisfied only with a continual desire to grow toward perfection in Christ – and is willing to put forth some personal effort to reach that goal. How fruitful he will be, for it will be God who is at work in his life.

Let us pause for a few moments at this juncture and refresh our minds regarding the process of justification and sanctification. The reason for this will become apparent momentarily. As discussed earlier in this study, justification is based on the finished work of Christ on behalf of mankind and our faith in the historic fact that he died that we might be united with God. Thus, justification deals with our past guilt and sin, providing for a process for removing them from our lives, thus enabling us to be in an ongoing relationship and constant communion with God. Justification is a "*once* for all times and all peoples" work of Christ. All have the opportunity, whether they ever make use of it or not, to be freely and equally justified in Christ.

Sanctification, on the other hand, is also the work of Christ in our lives but only as we respond in faith to him and the work of his Spirit within our lives. When we were confronted with the will of God and the principles of his governance over us, we soon realized that we could not live up to such a holy will and principles of such divine perfection and bear the necessary fruit in our own strength and goodness. We need something to put us over the edge, and that is the power of God at work in us. As we are justified by faith (faith in Christ's work on the cross), we are also sanctified by faith (faith in the power of the Holy Spirit within) (see 1 John 5:4). Whereas justification deals with the guilt and power of past sin in our lives, sanctification deals with the present power of sin as it strives to recapture us and once more distance our lives from God. There is a major difference beyond this simple observation, however. Justification is *once* for all, whereas sanctification is *moment by moment.*

At a definite point in time in the past we obeyed the gospel call of Christ and were at that moment justified by our faith response (cf. Rom. 5:1). We thereafter cease our concern about the business of justification, for it is the work of God on our behalf. In Christ we are justified and delivered from the wrath of God (cf. Rom. 5:9). Justification opens the way to a new life of peace with God, access to his grace, and confidence in hope. It is now an accomplished fact in our lives and the entranceway into the Christian walk. So, all of this having been said, now we must move on to the implications of such high-sounding theological concepts in our day-to-day existence, implications which involve the "down and dirty" business of sanctification, where the rubber meets the road, so to speak, the growing process whereby the Christian develops more and more toward spiritual maturity. Justification is a concept and a theological doctrine we do not worry about, for it is plainly outside the purview of our own activity, since it is the finished work of Christ. Sanctification, however, is something about which we ought to be deeply and consistently concerned. We fear that we are not growing. We face the future with such disturbing fears and anxious doubts. We do not have the confident assurance of present sanctification like we do of past justification. How can we overcome this troubling worry? We overcome such fears and doubts by realizing that the Christian life is lived *moment by moment*!

It is this wonderful *moment by moment* aspect of Christian living that we wish to give some consideration to at this point in our investigation. The purpose of this aspect of the study is to assist us in understanding on a more profound level the fact that sanctification, like justification, is a religious doctrine and a philosophical concept that we can also be assured of and comforted in, and appreciate that it, too, can prove to be in a sense "once for all." The reason we can say this is due to the fact that life is only a succession of all too quickly passing moments, taken just one moment at a time. Life is not a once-for-all thing, but rather a series of events or happenings. We can only live the Christian life moment by moment, and, therefore, we are sanctified from moment to moment. Just as an individual's justification took place at one moment in time, so one's sanctification is a moment by moment process. The past is past, the future is future, and the present is always now! The individual in Christ stands sanctified now! This is the precise teaching of the apostle John: "If we walk in the light [or *faith*], as he is in the light, we have fellowship with one another, and the blood of Jesus his Son cleanses[1] us from all sin" (1 John 1:7). At every individual moment in time, when we are walking in the light of God's eternal Word, we are continually sanctifying ourselves, productively bearing fruit, and thus not quenching, resisting, or grieving the Spirit. At every individual moment in time, we are faithfully trusting in God's promises. And it is during these tiny little slices of life, these individual moments of existence, that we are called upon to have believed with all of our hearts in the truthfulness and veracity of God's precious promises, respond to his providential will for us and to the urgings of his Spirit, and so allow the fruit of the Spirit to proceed from our lives.

Now, we do not want to leave the impression here that sanctification is an on-again, off-again type of life, that we are perpetually in a state of flux, sanctified one moment and unsanctified the next. As John teaches in 1 John 1:7, we stand continually in a saved and sanctified relationship with God as long as we are striving to do his will and are maintaining our faith and trust. What this means is that we do not have to worry continuously concerning the status of our faith and what it was yesterday, this morning, or even tomorrow. In Christ we have the comforting assurance that right now, at this very

---

[1] Greek present indicative active – "continually cleanses."

moment, we stand justified and sanctified before a loving and merciful God, as we persist in believing in his promises and respond to him by surrendering our lives to the promptings of his Spirit as his implanted Word influences us without and within.

This brings up another relevant and very pertinent question: if sanctification is a one-time action from moment to moment in our lives, what does this say in regards to what might be described as "degrees of sanctification"? Earlier in this book we stated simplistically that sanctification is more or less the Christianizing of the Christian, a gradual growth process, and, therefore, is manifested in varying degrees of maturity in different lives. If this is true, how can we say that sanctification is a "once for all" reality in our lives? The following thoughts should help to clarify this question. When we emphasize the "once for all" aspect of sanctification, we don't mean to imply that it is not a growth process, or that sanctification, in relation to its necessity for salvation, is something which exists only moment by moment in our life. In Christ, we continually stand sanctified, and thereby are continually in a saved relationship with God. Every faithful Christian, wherever he or she may be on the scale of sanctification or spirituality, is in a saved relationship with God. It is in this sense that sanctification is a "once for all" or moment by moment process. This does not mean that we will not continue to grow spiritually or for that matter draw ever nearer to the Lord in personal intimacy; rather it assures us that we can continually remain in a sanctified relationship with God. In the words of the apostle John, "I write this to you who believe in the name of the Son of God, that you may know that you have eternal life" (1 John 5:13). In Christ we have the assurance that we stand always justified and sanctified by God.

From this emphasis we ought to realize that the Christian faith is not a leap in the dark. It is not faith in a faith, but rather a believing and trusting faith in the reality of the one true and living God. The Christian faith is never without content because it is grounded upon the most profound principle of religious truth in the entire universe, namely, the finished redemptive work of God's Christ on the cross. It does indeed entail a moment by moment process of spiritual growth and sanctification. As we have attempted over and over to emphasize, this faith is not a legalistic, mechanical route toward spirituality, either. We ought never to urge individuals to read "x" number of chapters in the Bible each day, or to worship "x" number of times each week, or to pray "x" number of times each day, in order to realize the goal of true spiritual maturity. The Christian life is not a life composed of a set number of mechanical acts or of scripted rote rituals. It is a joyous moment by moment response to God's loving will for me and a moment by moment surrender of my inward and outward self to the indwelling Spirit of God. Genuine biblical and personal faith is a whole-hearted willingness to believe, obey, and be led by the Sprit of God, not just at the time when I initially became a Christian, not just during the happy times or at the good periods of my life, not just when I feel deeply spiritual, but at every moment in my life.

Discussion Questions

1. After examining your personal life, describe the ways in which you fulfill the apostle Paul's charge to "bear fruit for God" (Rom. 7:4). _____

   _____

   _____

2. How can Stephen's charge against the Jews, that being the sin of "resisting the Holy Spirit" (Acts 7:51), be a possibility for Christians today? _____

   _____

   _____

3. What does Jesus' word, "Blessed are those who hunger and thirst for righteousness" (Matt. 5:6), say about our personal spiritual development? _____

   _____

   _____

4. Comment. The Christian life is a "moment by moment" way of life in relation to sanctification, which is in contrast to the "once for all times" concept of justification.

XI. The Christian and Moral Guilt

In the previous chapters of this book we have emphasized the universality of the need of man to be freed from his persistent bondage to sin. Paul teaches in the Letter to the Romans that man, created in the image and glory of God, has fallen short of his true character and ultimate potential. The apostle wrote: "All have sinned and fall short of the glory of God" (Rom. 3:23). From this simple but profoundly accurate statement we are led to understand that whatever distinctions there may be in men, as viewed by the world, such factors vanish in the sight of God, for in this one area there is no distinction. All men, without exception or discrimination, are in the category of sinners as they stand in the presence of God (cf. Rom. 3:9-12). But we have also seen that man was made for a meaningful type of existence different from this unwholesome kind of life which he has tended to pursue, and that God has provided man with a means to realize such a beneficial and happy lifestyle. In Christ, God has redeemed, justified, and sanctified the obedient believer. When an individual, who has previously lived in the world and outside of communion with God and Christ, responds to God in obedient faith, he establishes a relationship with God - a relationship based on trust which, in turn, inevitably results in the bearing of fruit in that believer's life. Listen again to the apostle Paul as he explains the matter in greater detail:

> Since all have sinned and fall short of the glory of God, they are justified by his grace as a gift, through the redemption which is in Christ Jesus, whom God put forward as an expiation by his blood, to be received by faith. This was to show God's righteousness, because in his divine forbearance he had passed over former sins; it was to prove at

the present time that he himself is righteous and that he justifies him who has faith in Jesus (Rom. 3:23-26).

By one supreme act, in and through his glorious work on the cross, Christ broke the bonds which entrapped man and so freed the human family from such unpleasant bondage. The result of this work of Christ is that God is enabled to receive man and treat him as righteous. Through the cross, God has taken the initiative and done for man what man could never have done for himself.

At this juncture in our investigation of this subject it is important for us to concentrate on the results of God's work on our behalf in relation to our personal lives, especially as it pertains to the freedom we have from the bondage of sin. It is essential for us to recognize that, beyond the broader theological implications of the doctrine of Christian redemption, it is in fact the real and altogether aggravating presence of sin in our individual lives which is the thing that has caused such bondage to plague humanity. Sin not only separates us from God, it enslaves us. It not only alienates us from God, it brings us into captivity. It is not merely an unfortunate outward act or habit; it is a deep-seated inward corruption. Man is not just the victim of sin, either; he is a sinner by willful and deliberate intention. He turns away from what is right because he desires to have something which is not best for him and which will ultimately destroy him. Sin reveals a deep spiritual disease which grips the very heart of man. In recent years, secular man has tried to rid himself of the sense of sin and its accompanying guilt. He has duped himself into believing that mankind is improving and becoming better and better with the passing of time and the advancement of technology. But our Lord assured us that, all of this aside, we are historically and habitually enslaved to the practice of sin, "Truly, truly, I say to you, every one who commits sin is a slave to sin" (John 8:34). Paul, likewise, addressed himself to this same truth:

> Do you not know that if you yield yourselves to any one as obedient slaves, you are slaves of the one whom you obey, either of sin, which leads to death, or of obedience, which leads to righteousness? But thanks be to God, that you who were once slaves to sin have become obedient from the heart to the standard of teaching to which you were committed (Rom. 6:16-17; cf. Eph. 2:1-5; Titus 3:3).

The power of sin to conquer the souls of men is evident due to the fact that human love and kindness seem so rare in the world today. Hatred and suspicion have separated millions in this supposedly "progressive" age. It is sin that prevents man from portraying and effectively bearing the lifestyle and image of God. What we need, then, is a spiritual power to enable us to be freed from such bondage. We need a power to conquer and control self, a power to give us real moral character. Where do we turn for this power, and if it is possible to discover it, how do we act upon the resulting spiritual freedom and dynamic energy which helps us to escape from our hindering bondage to sin?

Prior to probing more deeply for the answers as to how we might achieve possible freedom from the bondage to sin in which all men appear to be ensnared, two things must be realized. The first of these is the fact that we must be genuine in our desire for such freedom. So many are satisfied with being average in commitment and sub-par in their devotion to the Lord that it is clear they do not really aspire to higher spirituality. In contrast to this, we must have the right kind of spiritual appetite in order to gain freedom from sin's bondage. The result of an improper and underdeveloped spiritual appetite is spiritually undernourished individuals. One indication of illness or disease being present in the body is loss of appetite. Similarly, something is very wrong if we are not hungry for that which helps us to develop and mature spiritually. God, however, has provided us with the means to overcome this problem, a means that not only delivers us from spiritual undernourishment, but one that also encourages in us a normal appetite and thus sound spiritual health. It is this means that leads us to the second thing we must come to realize in our quest to overcome our stubborn bondage of sin. What we have in mind here is the realization that we must act with energetic dispatch upon the biblical teachings concerning the acquisition of freedom from the bonds of sin.

Many of us have been taught since the early stages of our lives, even as early as Sunday school or Vacation Bible School, that God has the power to cleanse us of sin and moral guilt, and so we have come to accept that principle on the face of it. What we fail to realize many times, however, is that enjoying the benefits of such cleansing is not as simple as just hearing about the word of forgiveness and thereafter enjoying God's amazing grace without any effort on our part. This redemptive power of God must be actively sought and properly internalized by the individual believer. In the realm of spiritual healing, like all other healing, there must be a preparation which will then allow the power of God to operate effectively in our lives.

We have spent some time earlier in this book exploring the reality of the spiritual world in our universe. This spiritual world which we have come to experience since being joined to God and Christ in spiritual communion is just as real and powerful as the natural world we inhabit ordinarily. We have also discussed the reality of the spiritual powers available to us in Christ, powers which make it possible for the trustful believer to enjoy a saving relationship with the Godhead. We can therefore be spiritually nourished and become possessors of a wonderful salvation relationship with God at all times if we are continuously striving to walk in the light of God's truth and in the faith of our Lord Jesus Christ. This assurance is found everywhere in the scriptures, almost on every page of the New Testament, but it is especially emphasized in John's first epistle:

> If we walk in the light, as he is in the light, we have fellowship with one another, and the blood of Jesus his Son cleanses us from all sin....Every one who believes that Jesus is the Christ is a child of God, and every one who loves the parent loves the child. By this we know that we love the children of God, when we love God and obey his commandments. For this is the love of God, that we keep his commandments. And his commandments are not burdensome. For whatever is born of God overcomes the world; and this is the victory that overcomes the world, our faith....I write this to you who believe in the name of the Son of God, that you may know that you have eternal life. (1 John 1:7; 5:1-4, 13)

We have spiritual powers, the assurance of salvation, and the guarantee of the comforting presence of a personal, infinite God in whose image we are made. These things, contrary to what the world says, are *real* and they are available to all believers. So it is easily within our reach for us to grow beyond the bounds of what we may ever have thought possible: we *can* be spiritually mature. We must, however, act in the light of this potential, motivated by trusting faith and observant, submissive obedience on the foundational fact of these great truths. When we do this, then and only then will we be prepared so that God's power might be able to assert itself within us and act mercifully and beneficially in freeing us from the bondage to sin.

There is yet another situation which ought to be addressed at this time. At the point of our conversion to Christ and the resulting freedom from sin, we also must deal with the issue of moral guilt. The intriguing dilemma of the human condition, and of the modern twenty-first century man, in spite of his emphatic denials to the contrary, is two-fold: moral guilt and sin. We are speaking not just of guilt feelings, but of the existence and presence of real moral guilt and demonstrably real moral sin. Contrary to the prevalent thinking of twenty-first century philosophy and psychology, sin and guilt are as real as any physical malady that troubles the human family. Man has sinned against his Creator and Lord, a Creator and Lord who is in the essence of his very being holy and perfectly good. And it is this fact that makes sin and moral guilt so devastatingly real. The scriptures place strong emphasis on God's sovereignty and holiness. God is the One who is inexpressibly exalted and the One whose ethical holiness is set forth in perfect contrast with man's prevalent practice and persistent lifestyle. No matter how well one might keep the rules of morality, or how well one might attempt by his own pitiful efforts to purify himself, he remains unclean in the presence of God's total otherness, his unexcelled holiness.

Even a casual reading in the area of practical morality, as these principles are set forth by God in his Old and New Testaments and in the model of the perfect spiritual life illustrated by his Son, will make one ever more keenly aware of his own sinfulness and the lofty righteousness of God and Jesus Christ. The vision of God which portrayed his majesty and unique holiness, seen in the final year of King Uzziah's reign, made a great impact on the aspiring young prophet Isaiah. After having seen this ineffable vision of God, Isaiah was moved to this humble confession, "Woe is me! For I am lost; for I am a man of unclean lips, and I dwell in the midst of a people of unclean lips; for my eyes have seen the King, the Lord of hosts!" (Isa. 6:5). The holiness of God revealed to Isaiah the tremendous separation that existed between a holy God and an unholy humanity. The prophet's shocked and startled reaction in the presence of the pure and holy God was an admission of great moral uncleanness. He realized that he and all his people, regardless of how they might have viewed themselves as having fulfilled the legal requirements of the law, were in every sense a corrupt people, profoundly separated from what is holy. Isaiah later writes, "Your iniquities have made a separation between you and your God, and your sins have hid his face from you so that he does not hear" (Isa. 59:2).

What we gain from this is the understanding that man stands truly guilty before a holy God who dwells in the hallowed halls of a perfect heaven and against whom man has grossly sinned and deeply offended his majesty. Sin and moral guilt are not convenient inventions of preachers to keep themselves in a job; they are a universal fact attested throughout the Scriptures (cf. 1 Kings 8:46; Eccl. 7:20; Psa. 14:1-3; 130:3; 143:2; Isa. 53:6; 64:6; Rom. 3:22-23; 1 John 1:8, 10). The Sacred Writings view guilt and sin in the context of the individual's relationship to God. The result of sin is a defective and errant state in which an individual finds himself in his relationship to this holy God. Like the first human pair in the Garden of Eden, he finds himself embarrassed and deeply ashamed. Not only are sin and moral guilt a reality known by revelation, but they are also facts of our own personal everyday experience at home, on the job, and in the community. Try as we may to live right and do that which is good, a profound ambiguity between good and evil permeates everything we do. The awareness of this undeniable ambiguity is what produces our knowledge and awareness of separation from God. Unless we honestly come to grips with this and our need of deliverance from such, the hope given in the Scriptures concerning freedom from the bonds of sin is only a cruel illusion.

The good news that we have from God, however, is that we do not have to remain in a state of sinfulness and moral guilt because a way of victory has been won for us. The tenacious dark shadow of sin and moral guilt in our lives can be removed and will be erased from our conscience if we will but surrender to the will of God for us. Isaiah stood before the Lord fully aware of his moral sin and guilt, and deeply ashamed both of himself and of his people. Yet God said to him, "Behold...your guilt is taken away, and your sin is forgiven" (Isa. 6:7). Prior to this cleansing, Isaiah was morally inadequate, but now the penitent and forgiven Isaiah was assured of divine acceptance and ready to do service for his Lord. Convicted of his sin and moral guilt, made a beneficiary of God's grace, and empowered for a prophetic ministry by God, Isaiah was now victorious over the bonds of sin due to the forgiveness of God extended to him on this occasion to prepare him for his important mission.

As God freed Isaiah from his moral inadequacy, so he frees us from such by the sacrifice of his Son for our transgressions. From the time of Adam and Eve onward, everything pertaining to the regeneration of the human family rests on the finished work of God on the cross in Christ Jesus. It is not we who have personally brought ourselves down the path to victory or sanctification, but rather Jesus Christ. The apostle Paul also assures us of our bountiful access to this glorious triumph: "No temptation has overtaken you that is not common to man. God is faithful, and he will not let you be tempted beyond your strength, but with the temptation will also provide the way of escape, that you may be able to endure it" (1 Cor. 10:13). We have the immediate presence and continual helpfulness of the Spirit of God in order that we may benefit from and enjoy the "victory that overcomes the world" (1 John 5:4). Once more, let it be frankly and freely acknowledged that it is not our victory; it is Christ's victory, but – thanks be to God - we can share in it.

Once an individual obeys the gospel of Christ and is united with God through Christ, he begins living in the light of all that God has done for him and gives to him. The individual believer starts his journey toward spiritual maturity as he walks in the light of Christ. But what happens when sin makes its presence felt in our lives again? For some reason or other, no doubt associated with the inner acknowledgement of his own weakness and realization that he has failed the Lord again, the believer's faith and trust in God weakens. That special something that he used to possess in Christ is not there as strongly as it was at first. The peace, the self-confidence, the assurance of forgiveness, and that strong relationship to God – these things become cloudy when we slip and sin from time to time. Is the believer lost again? Has he relinquished all that he has formerly gained? Was all of his former faithfulness wasted in a single slip of the tongue or act of negligence? How can this be if justification was the work of Christ on behalf of the believer, a work performed once for all times? Surely this cannot be the case. Yet many times, as we look closely at our lives, we don't see manifested within our lives that victory in Christ demonstrated in practical application, or at least it may not seem to us as real as it used to be. What has happened? The good we know we ought to do goes undone, and we have somehow been cajoled into doing the evil we have learned to hate (cf. Rom. 7:15-25). We are caught in a battle between good and evil.

It is at this point in our lives of spiritual growth that we must realize the threat of and avoid at all costs the destructive effects of erosive discouragement. We must objectively and unemotionally analyze the situation and realize that we are very probably at one of those leveling-off junctions in our life of linear growth in spirituality. Or it may just be that we have actually suffered a *temporary* setback. We discussed earlier (cf. chapter IX) that sanctification is a gradual growth process, comparable to a broken, but upwardly inclined plane. Sometimes we are up, sometimes level, and sometimes even down, for sanctification deals with the power of sin in our lives and God's work in us to destroy that power. All in all, though, the direction of movement should be upward. In this situation we realize anew that sin is a real and a destroying power within us. The resulting tension within our lives between the power of sin and the work of God is the thing that produces the ups and downs in our spiritual growth. But what about the down times in our spiritual lives? Once we find ourselves in a decline, is there any way to turn this around? The answer is an unequivocal, "Yes!"

One of the grand things about the word of God is that it deals with man and the world as they really are, not as they ought to be. Our Creator and Lord is intensely aware of the insidious nature of sin and the fact that we sometimes feel powerless in our efforts to fight against sin alone. We lack the character and reliability to control such an awesome and destructive power. As this powerful enemy continually batters our puny personal defenses, we begin to level off, even occasionally to decline, and start to lose our sense of the image and awareness of God. God knows this; he knows there will be such times in our lives, times when we do not grow spiritually as we should, times when we go through periods in life when we are not what we might ought to be. If we exercise our faith in him, it is in these very situations that God will come through for us providing for us a way to make it through such crises and resume our quest for spiritual maturity. We may not escape the fight, but we can escape total defeat by the power of God's ever-present help, and we can realize the way to eventual victory. The basis for this, just as with justification and sanctification, is our confirmed trust in and dependency upon the finished work of Christ on the cross for our sins. The pathway which leads us out of any spiritual decline is plainly revealed by the apostle John in his First Epistle:

This is the message we have heard from him and proclaim to you, that God is light and in him is no darkness at all. If we say we have fellowship with him while we walk in darkness, we lie and do not live according to the truth; but if we walk in the light, as he is in the light, we have fellowship with one another, and the blood of Jesus his Son cleanses us from all sin. If we say we have no sin, we deceive ourselves, and the truth is not in us. If we confess our sins, he is faithful and just, and will forgive our sins and cleanse us from all unrighteousness (1 John 1:5-9).

There is hope for us in our conflict with sin. We must realize this and then act on that hope. Such hope, however, is dependent upon knowledge of the truth; it lies in our recognition that sin is a most powerful enemy. To admit this is to face the necessity for discovering the method of attack and God's ways and methods laid out for us in his Word to conquer the ferocious monster that is sin. When we are serious about this, there is assurance of victory. Take it lightly, and we shall also fall with the innumerable hosts of victims who have failed to see it for the beast that it is.

In the passage cited above (1 John 1:5-9), John assures his readers that God is light. In the Greek text, the phrase "in him is no darkness" (vs. 5) is a radically emphatic statement which contains two negatives. Principally, the phrase reads like this: "in him is no, not even one tiny particle of darkness." If God is light, that is, the source and essence of holiness and righteousness, goodness and truth, then those who live in fellowship with God will, out of moral and spiritual necessity, tend naturally to reflect his character and image in their lives. John assures us of this in his gospel: "He who does what is true comes to the light, that it may be clearly seen that his deeds have been wrought in God" (John 3:21). To walk in light requires honesty in facing up to our own inadequacies and genuineness in our dealings with God. It requires acknowledgement and confession of sin coupled with a sincere striving to shun sin in all of its forms. This means that we must stop explaining away or excusing sin when we encounter it in our own lives or in the lives of those whom we favor. We must face up to and confess sin and then overcome it with the all-sufficient powers of God which have been made so freely available to us. God is light and will illuminate and enrich the lives of those who are in genuine fellowship with him. But again, how can these things be true in our lives if we are facing or experiencing a period of spiritual decline? How is it possible for us to reflect his character and image in our lives when we seem not to be what we want to be, used to be, or in discouragement, feel we are not what we can be? The fact remains and ought not be avoided, that we cannot walk in darkness and be in fellowship with the light of God.

It is not possible for us to truly reflect the character and image of God as we might wish if we are trapped in a period of spiritual decline. It is possible, however, for us to come out of this tendency toward spiritual decadence: if only we will take a few simple action steps: "If we confess our sins, he is faithful and just, and will forgive our sins and cleanse us from all unrighteousness" (1 John 1:9). The blood of Christ does not prevent us from sinning, but it does establish and maintain our fellowship with God by removing all guilt of sin (cf. 1 John 1:7). As we strive to reflect the image and character of Christ in our lives, God will cleanse us from whatever sin that would otherwise mar our relationship with him. But again, even though a Christian may be in a spiritually immature state, we surely do not desire to remain in such a condition. We want to come out of any period of spiritual decline and rise to a higher level of spirituality. We want to better reflect the image and character of God. But how is it possible for us to break this downward spiral and rise again to new heights of spirituality? We do so by admitting to God that we are not what we should be or can be and by coupling this with an urgent request for him to help and empower us so that we may be more like what he desires us to be. We do not deny, nor minimize, the fact of our sin. That would be the worse conceivable option. We must not call our failure by another name, or blame someone else, or call it by a name that somehow defines it as something less than sin. We must honestly and openly confess our shortcomings, repent of them in godly sorrow, and thankfully appropriate God's provision for our cleansing and restoration. That is the road to spiritual restoration as outlined by John, and we ought gladly to take it lest we "fail to obtain the grace of God" (Heb. 12:15) because of our own obstinacy and unwillingness to yield to the Lord's corrective discipline.

We need to emphasize at this time that the individual Christian will never acquire the character and image of God as a perfect and permanent possession. The Lord God is holy and majestic, one whose nearness excites the greatest wonder and the most awesome dread. We will never stand before God as a finished product by our own achievements or through our own efforts alone; instead, we will always be as it were "under construction" or, if you will, engaged in a process of perfecting. We will also always be dependent on the gracious forgiveness and cleansing of a faithful and righteous God. Man is not an autonomous being but a creature whose very existence rests on the fact that God cares and is involved intimately with him. Ethical living and freedom from the bondage of sin are dependent upon the continuous blessing of this merciful and caring God who has revealed what is just and what is good and then empowers us through his grand and glorious Spirit to achieve such an auspicious goal in our lives. The very possibility of this as an obtainable objective is not because God is indulgent and easygoing. For us to view it so we would have to ignore the stark reality of the cross and the death of our Lord. Rather it is because God is everlastingly faithful to his promise and so is righteous in his acquittal of the confessing believer: "If we confess our sins, he is faithful and just, and will forgive our sins and cleanse us from all unrighteousness" (1 John 1:9).

This, then, is the means that God uses to deal with his children who have fallen and desire be restored to his fellowship and rise again to a higher lifestyle. But what happens to an individual who is in a low spiritual state and decides to stay in that situation? Is not this a situation that warrants and in the end motivates God to disciplinary action? As a Father, God chastises his children due to his love for them. God's ideal for his children is that they should be perfected spiritually just as he is perfect. He will not take into his company any person, however seemingly orthodox in life and mind, who will not strive to follow after a pattern of holiness in his life. And furthermore, those whom he does accept, he exposes to discipline in order that they might move ever closer to perfect holiness and so attain a more distinct likeness to his Son. Without such chastisement, we would not be children of God. This is the very thing that the writer of the Epistle to the Hebrews teaches:

> My son, do not regard lightly the discipline of the Lord, nor lose courage when you are punished by him. For the Lord disciplines him whom he loves, and chastises every son whom he receives. It is for discipline that you have to endure. God is treating you as sons; for what son is there whom his father does not discipline? If you are left

without discipline, in which all have participated, then you are illegitimate children and not sons. Besides this, we have had earthly fathers to discipline us and we respected them. Shall we not much more be subject to the Father of spirits and live? For they disciplined us for a short time at their pleasure, but he disciplines us for our good, that we may share his holiness. For the moment all discipline seems painful rather than pleasant; later it yields the peaceful fruit of righteousness to those who have been trained by it (Heb. 12:5b-11).

Did not Jesus also say, "Those whom I love, I reprove and chasten" (Rev. 3:19)? Jerome, the great religious writer and Bible translator of the fourth century, said, "The greatest anger of all is when God is no longer angry with us when we sin." Jerome seems to have meant by this cryptic remark that our greatest punishment would be that of being abandoned to our sin as a hopeless reprobate. God will not do this, however, unless we completely close our hearts to him. He will discipline us as sons and the very purpose of such discipline is "that we may share his holiness" (Heb. 12:10). God's will for us is our sanctification, which is the predetermined condition and most essential constituent of our happiness, not only in this life, but also in life hereafter.

The clue to understanding all God's dealings with us is this: throughout life God is training us for the future that awaits us. He is, so to speak, fashioning us as an artful potter meticulously shapes his clay into the image of his Son. In Christ we are brought to the stature of sons of God, to a faint semblance of a child of God, by God's alternating efforts at discipline and redemption. In fact the very word "discipline" is obviously and intimately related to the word "disciple," not only linguistically, but also spiritually. Thus, discipline is a certain mark of spiritual sonship. It reveals God's holy wisdom and his filial benevolence toward us as his children. Its absence in our lives would be a sure sign of disinheritance.

In order to produce the fruits of the Spirit and grow in spirituality, then we must be constantly experiencing the various chastisements of God. The disciple must be learning by this sometimes mysterious process what the Father is teaching us in the midst of life. If we fail to understand it as such, then we will lack an appreciation for what he is trying to do for us and in us. In the same context, it is imperative that we also live a life of confession: "Confess our sins" (1 John 1:9), says John. And what we must realize here is that the admission that we are sinners is not sufficient, nor is it even what he has in mind when he makes this statement. It costs so very little to say that we are sinners, for this means no more than an admission that we are like everybody else. On the other hand, the confession of particular sins which we have committed costs the ego a great deal and is the ultimate assurance of our genuineness and sincerity. We must also avoid the tendency to blame our sins on our special situation in life, our particular heredity or our unique temperament, or even to blame others who we may claim to have led us astray. We must acknowledge that we are sinners (cf. Rom. 3:23), by both practice and free-will. This is often so difficult that we may be tempted to resist, but it is the point where we begin to experience the meaning of yielding wholly to the will of God – what Christ encountered in the Garden of Gethsemane: "Not as I will, but as thou wilt" (Matt. 26:39). We must say with reference to the cross, or crosses, in our lives, "Father, I want your will to be done in my life, not my own will." Sin, which keeps us from intimacy with God, is the result of willfulness, pride, and selfishness. Moreover, these attitudes not only lead to sin; in themselves they are sin. We must stop attempting, as so many do, to be a diminutive god for ourselves, lay aside our pride, and allow God's will to be our real goal in life.

The parable of the prodigal son (cf. Luke 15:11-24) is a good illustration of an individual who wanted to direct his own affairs and not live in the will of his father The young man foolishly thought he knew all about life. He wanted to live life fully and live it on his own terms without any interfering advice from his father or anyone else. The prodigal began his downward spiral in self-will, but, as we realize in this parable, self-will always becomes blind; it mars one's life and sends it off the cliff into tragedy. The younger son found himself deeply involved in sin, and not just the "little" sins either, but the "big" sins. By recklessly seeking to assert himself and be independent, he had betrayed his deepest purpose in life and so had brought himself to ruin. The good news, however, is that the story did not end there; at the last he came to himself, approached his father with an attitude of repentant humility, and was restored: "Father, I have sinned against heaven and before you." The wonderful part of the story then touchingly follows: "His father saw him and had compassion, and ran and embraced him and kissed him." He had originally left his father's side arrogant and self-sufficient. He came back in deep humility making his earnest confession, and yet it is clear that all the while his father had but one thing in mind for him – sonship!

The spiritual parallel of this parable is simple and readily evident to the thoughtful reader: the blood of Christ and the love of God can cleanse us from the darkest of sins if we humbly recognize the sin, call it what it is, and, through trusting and obedient faith, bring it under the saving work of Jesus Christ. We must realize that our Father in heaven also suffers when we are involved in sin and separation from him is the uncomfortable but inevitable result. In the comforting arms of our sin, we may not realize the depths of our separatedness, but God never ceases to realize the breadth of this horrible separation. On the basis of the decisive spiritual victory won for us by Christ, however, we never have to live life in the negative. The founding principle of this is not a theological doctrine or a philosophical theory; rather it is the finished work of Christ on the cross and the objective promises of God that are found in his word. If we believe his verbal commitments and trust implicitly in him, and if we have complete confidence in what he has confirmed concerning the sufficiency of the work of his Son for our restoration, we can have assurance and freedom from moral guilt for past failures. Such is the result of God's love, admittedly, not love that we deserve, but love that we assuredly need, and love without which life would be mostly futile and meaningless.

Understanding all this, however, does not relieve us of all of the problems that we might otherwise encounter in life. For example, what do we do about our conscience which is often so troublesome to us? We would expect that the salvation we enjoy in Christ should also include salvation from a guilty conscience. It is both natural and right that our consciences become evermore tender when we become Christians, for this is the work of the Holy Spirit as he instructs us and fortifies us with knowledge from the written Word and so alters our very being from within. In many ways, one might even argue that the inner conflict between the good and the evil in our consciences is intensified (see Paul's conflict which he describes in Romans 7:15-25). One of the greatest activities of God in the personal lives of his disciples is his power to create a more delicate conscience in individual lives. God's will as revealed through a conscience that has been immersed in his word is often a lone guiding light in a sin-torn world. This does not mean, however, that we should be bowed down by agonizing guilt on our conscience week after week due to past sins and failures. We must not allow our conscience to make cowards of us all. Our conscience is not infallible, nor is it ever to be viewed as the infallible and ultimate criterion in the moral life. If we think our conscience is always right, then we would also have to say the court was right that condemned Socrates, that the early Catholic Church was right in its persecution of heretics, and so forth. Those who committed these great wrongs were also guided by their consciences, and it is clear from these and many other comparable illustrations that a wrongly taught conscience may not only lead us to do wrong, but may cause us to feel guilt even when our actual guilt has been erased by God's forgiveness. We know our conscience is not infallible. It is a helpful guide to the understanding of God's will, but only a proper guide when it is in harmony with that will. We need to be aware of the fact that the conscience is in need of continual education and especially in the truth of the forgiving and cleansing power of God and make the necessary provision to that end.

Once we become sensitive to the presence of sin in our lives and bring such sin to the divine font, the cleansing blood of Christ, it is forgiven and forgotten. That ought to be the end of it. To continue to worry about personal sin that has been repented of and forsaken would have the effect of discrediting the saving power of the work of Christ. The power of the gospel resides in the God-given assurance of our acceptance by him even though we are keenly aware of our past mistakes. The grace and love of God motivates him to remove our guilt and give us a new name – son of God! As with the prodigal son, we claim nothing and demand less, yet we receive everything. There may be a price yet to pay in regard to the effect of sin in our lives. Sin has repercussions in this world that divine forgiveness cannot erase or even diminish. Suffering and punishment often come as a direct consequence of our sins, suffering and punishment in what we may have experienced and in the scars that we will always wear. But as far as our relationship with God is concerned, when we have repudiated our sin and laid it at the foot of the cross, we are finished with it. We are united with the Father, Son, and Holy Spirit due to the life and sacrifice of our Lord and Savior on our behalf. As we rest in the knowledge of this fact, with faith and confidence in God's untiring love, our conscience should be at peace.

It is a hard thing to admit, but the truth of the matter is that we do sin and will continue to sin. The scriptures do not teach perfectionism. But just as true is the fact of sin forgiven, the fact that whatever sin we bring to Christ, in humility and sorrow, is forgiven: "My little children, I am writing this to you," says the apostle John, "so that you may not sin; but if any one does sin, we have an advocate with the Father, Jesus Christ the righteous" (1 John 2:1). John uses the present indicative verb, "have" (*echomen*), which means literally, "we keep on having." The promise to us is that we have an ever-present remedy, or advocate, for our sin. Our advocate does not plead that we are innocent; rather he acknowledges our guilt and then presents his vicarious suffering and death on the cross as the ground of our acquittal. The word "advocate" was used of a party who took one's side in a lawsuit or trial. Therefore, the magnificent good news is that we have more than a "Comforter;" we have a friend in our time of greatest need, "one called alongside" to intercede on our behalf.

In relation to forgiveness, we must mention one more aspect of this great gift, that being, our need of consistent personal discipline. Paul's words to the Christians at Corinth summarize this notion: "If we judged ourselves truly, we should not be judged. But when we are judged by the Lord, we are chastened so that we may not be condemned with the world" (1 Cor. 11:31-32). While this admonition is concerned, contextually and primarily, with the Lord's Supper, it is universally practical and applies equally well to other areas of life. The lesson here is that if we would learn to judge, or chasten, ourselves, the Lord would not need to discipline us. We grow in spirituality and grace as we give ourselves over fully to self-discipline – the discipline of study, of prayer, of fellowship, and of Christian service. We do not have to wait for the discipline of the Lord. We need only to develop the healthy habit of self-discernment and learn to distinguish between the good and the evil. Such a habit will assure us of a life of unswerving fellowship with God. This habit, too, involves discipline, for the old man must not only be put off once and for all, the new man must also be put on. This comes from a conscious and coherent effort to do the will of God. To live in such a manner will involve a life of self-judgment, cleansing, and renewal. The fact that the Lord has had to chasten us so often in the past is irrefutable evidence that we have not yet developed this trait of spiritual maturity. The lack of such is seen also in our ineffective and often clumsy modeling of the teachings of our Master to the world as his disciples, our frequently sluggish participation in worship, and our slackness in study and the rather extensive gaps in our biblical knowledge and growth.

We need to emphasize also that the chastisement of the Lord is not to be viewed as punishment for our sins. The punishment for sin has already been dealt with on the cross of Christ. This chastisement to which we have reference here is sent into our lives in love, in the form of gentle discipline designed for our own personal profit. The judgments of the Lord are not against us; rather they are evidences of fatherly love ("If you are left without discipline...then you are illegitimate children and not sons" – Heb. 12:8), not of consuming punitive wrath. The purpose of such discipline is to fill the gaps and fix the fissures in our lives and make us more what we ought to be. The special object of this chastisement is "that we may not be condemned along with the world" (1 Cor. 11:32b). As one has well said, "God troubles his people now, that he may not trouble them hereafter. He smites gently now, that he may not smite them with the arm of destruction." It is certainly true that self-discipline will not make us spiritual, but it will drive us away from sin and toward the power that can make us more truly spiritual. Self-discipline moves us to yield to God's word and thus allow his Spirit to work effectively within us.

One of the blessings Christian people enjoy in Christ is the exultant freedom from the rabid tyranny of a false or misinformed conscience. The basic first step to that wholeness of life so promised by God in Christ (cf. John 10:10) is the knowledge of the healing of that separation between man and God, a separation brought about due to individual sin (cf. Isa. 59:2). Being separated from God, man is thus also separated from himself and at war within himself, and in the end he is alienated with all the rest of the world also. The atoning death of Christ, however, has definitively healed this expansive and frightful breach. When we believe this divine promise in trusting faith, then and only then will we enjoy the quality of life God meant for us to have, that magnificent reality referred to by Jesus as "abundant life." Freedom from the hateful tyrannies of this world can be ours when our life is governed and permeated by the indwelling Spirit of Christ, instructed by the word of Christ, and delivered mightily from an impure conscience by the blood of Christ.

Discussion Questions

1. Society would have us to believe that humanity is in an upward movement to a higher morality and ethical lifestyle. How would you respond to this? _____

   _____

   _____

2. What is the believer to do, when sin again makes its presence felt in his or her life from time to time? _____

   _____

   _____

   _____

3. Is there ever a time in the Christian's spiritual development when he or she might expect and even value discipline from the Lord?_____

   _____

4. What is the downside in avoiding the confession of particular sins before God and falling into the habit of confessing general sins that is, confessing that I am a sinner without going into the details of particular sins? _____

   _____

   _____

   _____

5. Comment. To continue to worry about personal sin that has been repented of and forsaken would say what about the salvation work of Christ in my personal life?

XII. The Christian's Thought-Life

According to the inspired and profoundly thoughtful writer of Proverbs, "As [a man] thinketh in his heart, so is he" (Prov. 23:7, KJV). The basic attitudes a man holds true and dear within his heart, taken cumulatively, is the thing which largely determines whether life seems to him to be heavy and oppressive, or whether the individual rises above the plentiful difficulties he experiences to become spiritually triumphant. We know from the Holy Scriptures that God has always been concerned about a man's heart or mind (cf. Matt. 15:10-11, 15-20; 23:25-28; Phil. 4:8-9). He places very strong emphasis upon the motive behind every act contemplated and then acted upon by a man, and thus ultimately upon the thinking of his heart, for this is where all of life's activity originates. This concern is due to the fact that the heart or mind largely determines and dominates what a man will be – spiritually, mentally, and physically. In the scriptures, therefore, we find a special concern for the inward aspects of man. It is for this reason that the purpose of this chapter in our study is situated as it is here toward the end of the present work, in order to investigate the importance of the Christian's thought-life in his quest for spiritual maturity.

Up to this point in our study we have attempted to emphasize several important things, namely the importance of actually dying to self, of demonstrating to the world in real and tangible ways the spiritual realities in Christ, of the necessity of bearing the wonderful and desirable fruits of the Spirit, and the resulting freedom the joyous man in Christ has from the virtual hand-cuffs of guilt and moral sin. What needs to be emphasized in the quest for these things, however, is that success or failure in gaining spiritual maturity is subject to the condition of one's heart or mind. All external manifestations are the direct result of the internal thought-life. One individual undergoing essentially the same circumstances in life becomes a spiritually mature Christian; another becomes discouraged, despondent, and weak spiritually. Much of the final outcome in both situations depends upon the attitude of the fellow in question, in other words, his thought-life. The battle for spiritual maturity is going to be won first of all within our hearts and minds. John Allen put it well when he wrote, "A noble and God-like character is not a thing of favor or chance, but is the natural result of continued effort in right thinking, the effect of long cherished association with God-like thoughts. An ignoble and festival character, by the same process, is a result of the continuing harboring of groveling thoughts."[1]

It is not that we are saying that there is no merit in working out our salvation with good works (cf. Phil. 2:12). There is strong emphasis in the word of God about bearing fruit. It may be that we were able to succeed in the early stages of our Christian life by acting out and "going through the motions" in imitation of what we have learned through the careful practice of good works, but for the mature Christian the central thing is not merely outward activity but a right mind or heart set squarely on right principles, which will inevitable result in producing good works and a righteous character. Without a right heart, our good works will soon become merely heavy burdens and we will eventually cease doing them. The devotion of our thought-life to God, however, will transcend this tendency, as well as everything else. Conforming our wills to God's purpose, attending worship services, praying, and studying the Bible will result when our thought-life is intimately attuned to God as our partner and friend in life. Devotion to God, therefore, is not primarily a set of legal obligations; it is the wonderful expression of a love and concern for God manifested in our heart and mind.

Let us begin this aspect of our study by examining carefully the words of the apostle Paul to the church at Rome in Romans 1:18-32. In his powerful and penetrating words to the Roman Christians, the

---

[1] James Allen, *As A Man Thinketh*, quoted from *Baxter's Sermons*, No. 449, January 9, 1966.

apostle has been trying to drive home the unhappy truth that men are guilty before God, subject to the pernicious practice of and subsequent bondage of sin and totally incapable of saving themselves through obedience to God's law given through Moses as well as natural law as it existed in the various human societies throughout history. Attention is given to the moral failure of the Gentiles, then to that of the Jew. The truth of the matter, according to Paul, is that men have only tended to wander further away from the righteousness of God rather than achieve any level of genuine righteousness. What we have distilled and summarized here is the universality of the often unrealized but truly desperate need of man, "since all have sinned and fall short of the glory of God" (Rom. 3:23). Man, originally created in the image and glory of God, has historically and persistently fallen short of this true character. Why? What accounts for this devastating human failure? The answer to this question will become quickly apparent as we focus further on Paul's quiet emphasis on the internal world of a man's thought-life.

The first verse toward which we will direct our attention is Romans 1:21: It states: "For although they knew God they did not honor him as God or give thanks to him, but they became futile in their thinking and their senseless minds were darkened." Like many people whom we encounter in our world today, here were individuals who knew some true things about God, yet thoughtlessly turned aside from him because they lost all light and sense of direction. As a result, their thought-life became "futile" and "darkened" as they passed on to the next stage, into a proud and ungrateful disregard for God. "Claiming to be wise, they became fools" (vs. 22). Their thought-life was fundamentally wrong and the result of such petty thinking was that "God gave them up in the lusts of their hearts to impurity, to the dishonoring of their bodies among themselves" (vs. 24). When a man refuses to seek truth with intellectual honesty and integrity of heart, he is unable to reason or think clearly. He loses that inner morality that ought to be a part of every man. The result is that he completely loses his way in the world, and so he also in a sense "loses his mind", as he foolishly fabricates idols and worships and serves the creatures rather than the Creator. The natural man does not in his unredeemed state know God, not due to error of thought or experience, but due to a fundamentally wrong inward attitude – vanity of mind and blindness of heart. Here, then, is the simple order of man's fall from grace and fellowship with God: first there was the prevailing idea of rebellion and departure in his thought-life, and then came the outward results of that idea. Bereft of spiritual wisdom and thus of a proper thought-life and left to their own devices, men are at the mercy of the dominion of the excesses and outrages of the powers of the world. Thus, our outward conduct comes to be governed precisely by what we desire instead of what is best for us. By a strict inevitability we have reached the ill-advised and ill-fated goal we have set before ourselves in our thought-life.

This same truth is expressed in Romans 1:25 when Paul writes that the Gentiles "exchanged the truth about God for a lie and worshipped and served the creature rather than the Creator." This service to the creature began with Adam and Eve, even though they were commanded to "have dominion" (Gen. 1:26-27) over all creation. Not exercising the power they were given, they instead bowed to the deceptive and devastating advice of the serpent, thus giving over their thought-life and mind to this frail creature's advice. Paul reveals in Romans 1:24-25 that the inward rebellion of the thought-life brings about a wide variety of external evil results. In every life, one's thoughts are the rulers and real governors of all action, the formative principle of all personal life. In verse 28 also, "Since they did not see fit to acknowledge God, God gave them up to a base mind and improper conduct." Again, the external follows the internal. Thoughts are always first in time and priority then there follow their inevitable products, which in the end precipitate evil conduct being manifested externally. As the very unique existence of man's thought-life is the capacity that raises him far above the rest of God's creation, so it is that power if and when it is exercised properly which molds his character and fits him for eternity with God. Thus Paul's admonition to "take every thought captive to obey Christ" (2 Cor. 10:5) is essential advice for every child of God.

This same emphasis on the thought-life of man is brought to our attention again in Romans 12. Paul describes it in terms well known from both the Old Testament sacrificial system in Leviticus and in the pagan religions of the time. The life of an animal was taken, and its body draped across the altar as an offering whence it was burned. Here is given a whole new meaning: "I appeal to you therefore, brethren, by the mercies of God, to present your bodies as a living sacrifice, holy and acceptable to God, which is your spiritual worship" (vs. 1). This charge is to be carried out externally in our lives. As we have been stressing throughout this study, we are to cease living to ourselves in order that we may live to God and others. We must express in outward concrete action what the Lord would demand of us. But how is this outward lifestyle to become a reality? It is possible only if preceded by the right internal thought-life, for again, the external lifestyle is the eventual product of the internal thought processes. This is the exact thing that Paul says in the next verse of Romans 12: "Do not be conformed to this world but be transformed by the *renewal of your mind*, that you may prove what is the will of God, what is good and acceptable and perfect" (vs. 2). The true worship of God is to dedicate ourselves to him without reserve, but such dedication requires the uniting of the inner thought-life with the outer moral life. In Christ we have received the ability to prove, in every concrete situation, what God's will is for his holy people. We have received a new mind and a new way of thinking and judging; "we have the mind of Christ" (1 Cor. 2:16) and so can acutely discern that which is good and acceptable and perfect. We no longer judge according to the ways and means of the world that surrounds us on every side and wants so intently to redefine who we are and how we are to think. Our mind is set to do the will of God. We are always tempted however, to believe that we can effectively serve God outwardly by the simple and thoughtless multiplication of outward acts and ritual, but such is impossible if our thought-life is not first in harmony with God. The transformation of our thought-life is the key to the problem of right living. When our mind is renewed – a change of heart, mind, and attitude – then we are in the process of being transformed into that quality of life which leads to spiritual maturity.

Christians are not to be conformed to this age, but must live as if they are already participants in the new age to come. We have left behind us the old age and entered into the thought world of a new age. But our minds must not remain in the worn out pattern of the old, nor be conformed to the old. Our thought-life and accompanying conduct must be in harmony with the new age which we claim that we have embraced. To do this involves a complete reevaluation and reorientation which only the Spirit of God can bring to fruition. It is in essence a recreation of the thought-life so that, unlike the Jews and Gentiles of Romans 1:18-32, we are united in mind and action;

our minds being renewed – given new life and power. Paul wrote in Romans 7:21-25 and its context that on the one hand he serves the law of God with his mind, or "inmost self," but on the other that his "mind" is weak to resist the tendencies to sin in his flesh. He goes on to say, however, that there is good news in that our minds can be "renewed." Every activity of the Christian's life is an action that is brought into harmony with the will of God by a mind that is being re-newed by the Holy Spirit into conformity with the mind of Christ. And so we are brought back to consideration of the thought-life again. This transformation of thought is the key to solving the problem of ethical living, for it is the place where the turning about takes place by which we are directed toward a new type of lifestyle and behavior. And what is this but "repentance," for repentance means "change of mind" (*metanoia*)? So repentance, as the primary ethical action, is the key to rethinking, and rethinking is the key to ethical living. The renewing of the mind involves a repentance which extends beyond an inner change to a gradual transformation into that new spiritual relationship we share with God in Christ.

This emphasis on the thought-life as the controlling factor in one's moral life is underlined also in Paul's Ephesian epistle. The apostle writes, "Now this I affirm and testify in the Lord, that you must no lon-ger live as the Gentiles do, in the futility of their minds" (Eph. 4:17). This passage, just as the one written about the Gentiles of Rome (cf. Rom 1:18-32), reveals the *inward* reality of the sinfulness of the Gentile world. Paul goes on to say in the next verse that these Gen-tiles "are darkened in their *understanding*, alienated from the life of God because of the *ignorance* that is *in them*, due to their hardness of *heart*." Again, exactly as in Romans 1, the Ephesians' thought-life was at one time equally wrong and this in turn led to a darkening in their understanding which inevitably resulted in an external corrup-tion in terms of their lifestyle: "They have become callous and have given themselves up to licentiousness, greedy to practice every kind of uncleanness" (Eph. 4:19). This corruption originated as an inner cause, a darkened understanding, and it resulted in an outer mani-festation, a persistent and pernicious separation from and even avoidance of what is holy.

In sharp contrast to this worldly thought-life, Paul writes, "You did not so learn Christ" (Eph. 4:20). The complete thought of the apostle would be this: "You have not so learned Christ as to continue to think like the Gentiles; you have learned of him in such a manner that you will not fail to put off the old thought-life...." Notice here that learning Christ is also an internal reality; it is a matter of thoughts in a rational sense and thoughts freighted with content. Human nature cannot be reformed; it must be regenerated. The new, which replaces the old and gives the believer a type of righteousness kindred to that of Christ, takes place in the innermost being, deep within the spirit, and centered in the thought-life.

We gather from this that the Christian life is fundamentally a matter of controlling our thought-life. If we center our thinking and internal nature on Christ, moral battles will easily be won externally, and the explanation of and cause for such victories will be found in the internal world of one's thoughts. Since our mind exerts a dominating and steering power over the body and its actions, a mind attuned to God will mean that no less than a complete change of the total man will be forthcoming. The result of a mind in harmony with God is therefore a "new man in Christ."

The apostle Paul is not alone in his emphasis on the importance of having a correct thought-life in order to develop an outward spirituality. Our Lord also stressed this truth with great force. In speaking to the Pharisees, he said, "You brood of vipers! How can you speak good, when you are evil? For out of the abundance of the heart the mouth speaks" (Matt. 12:34). What Jesus is saying here is, that if we do not have the internal condition of our life right, our inward self, we cannot bring forth proper fruit. Listen to him as he further enunciates this truth:

> Not what goes into the mouth defiles a man, but what comes out of the mouth, this defiles a man....Do you not see that whatever goes into the mouth passes into the stomach, and so passes on? But what comes out of the mouth proceeds from the heart, and this defiles a man. For out of the heart come evil thoughts, murder, adultery, fornication, theft, false witness, slander. These are what defile a man; but to eat with unwashed hands does not defile a man (Matt. 15:11, 17-20).

A man's conduct in life, expressed in deeds and actions, is first of all an expression of his thought-life. If the heart or mind is not right with the Lord and in conformity with his will, there is no way to make the outward lifestyle what it ought to be in the sight of God. It is the thought-life that supersedes all else.

In the Sermon on the Mount, Jesus deals at some length with the principle that the only righteousness acceptable to God is that divine righteousness that in time brings about a full transformation of the inner character.

> You have heard that is was said to the men of old, "You shall not kill; and whoever kills shall be liable to judgment." But I say to you that every one who is angry with his brother shall be liable to judgment; whoever insults his brother shall be liable to the council, and whoever says, "You fool!" shall be liable to the hell of fire...." You have heard that it was said, "You shall not commit adultery." But I say to you that every one who looks at a woman lustfully has already committed adultery with her in his heart (Matt. 5:21-22, 27-28).

This teaching of Jesus is essentially repeated by the apostle John in slightly different wording when he writes, "Any one who hates his brother is a murderer" (1 John 3:15). While the human law which governs society considers only overt acts, God considers the motives in one's thought-life, for this is where all the outward acts of hatred, violence, and wickedness originate. The very heart of the Sermon on the Mount, which is itself the essence of the Christian message, is the insistence upon the need for this very step – the profound and important understanding that outer conformity, as absolutely essential as it is, is not sufficient in itself. If we are to mature spiritually, we have not merely to conform outwardly to the rules and ordinances of the faith; we must change the inner man as well. Anger, hatred, lust, indignation, resentment, and other wrong desires are all things that form an impenetrable barrier to spiritual maturity. Moreover, every single one of these vices has its origin in the heart.

Sin cannot therefore be defined in terms of actions and deeds only. It is an attitude of one's heart that in every instance stimulates an untoward act. The outward act itself is nothing more than the external symptom of the thoughts of the mind and heart, the inward malady. Any outward act is but the sequel to a thought, and the type of thought which we allow to become habitual will sooner or later find expression in action. The fact that one has not committed an overt act does not mean that he or she is without guilt before God; he may be innocent in a court of law, but before his Maker his thoughts may be provocative or even rebellious. Thus, the Proverb writer says, "Keep your heart with all vigilance; for from it flow the springs of life" (Prov. 4:23). It is not so much that an individual does a thing; it is also of concern what motivates him to do it. And when we try to control the thoughts of the heart, it is then that we realize both the importance of a right and proper thought-life and the tremendous power and depth of sin as it relentlessly encroaches not only one's life but the very private inner sanctum of his heart.

Up to this point in this section of our study we have advanced three propositions. First, the thought-life of the individual is the beginning point of all action, moral and immoral, in every individual life. Second, the external manifestations from the individual's life are the results of one's inner thinking. And third, the thought-life is the central consideration in regard to issues pertaining to morality because God considers the motives behind every action as central in importance. This is due to the fact that it is out of the thought-life that the outward acts of hatred, violence, and wickedness have their point of origin. Until we realize this truth, we will never find the strength or possess the wisdom to overcome our spiritual limitations. Thoughts are literally substantial mental phenomena and our outward conduct is finally determined by our choice of the kind of mental furniture that we permit to occupy the center of the stage of our mind. We must discover and come to appreciate the fundamental truth that a wrong thought is just as destructive an act as is a wrong deed.

A prime illustration of how wrong thoughts can lead to destructive deeds is found in the story of Joseph as it is recorded in Genesis 37. We note in this story proof positive that the internal thoughts were the things that led to the wrong acts described. We read of Joseph's brothers: "They hated [Joseph], and could not speak peaceably to him" (Gen. 37:4b). In the next verse we read, "Now Joseph had a dream, and when he told it to his brothers they only hated him more" (vs. 5). Yet a third time we read, "So they hated him yet more for his dreams and for his words" (vs. 8). And finally we read that "his brothers were jealous of him" (vs. 11). In this illustration we are led to conclude that the internal thoughts of hatred arose in the hearts of the brothers prior to their pitiless external evil deed. The brothers hated Joseph and this hatred motivated them to violate the commandments of God. Genesis records the events in the following way,

> They saw [Joseph] afar off, and before he came near to them they conspired against him to kill him. They said to one another, "Here comes this dreamer. Come now, let us kill him and throw him into one of the pits; then we shall say that a wild beast has devoured him, and we shall see what will become of his dreams" (Gen. 37:18-20).

These brothers were perfectly willing to kill their younger brother, break the heart of their elderly father, and do violence to God's law, and it is clearly evident that all this evil originated within the inner world of their thought-life. It was the hatred and envy within their thought-life that motivated the evil deed which they carried out externally. Their sin was not only in selling their brother into slavery. Their sin was centered in their thought-life. The outward deed was quite simply a direct consequence of an inward wrong.

This same truth is illustrated in the story of the fall of man in Genesis 3. We read that, "When the woman saw that the tree was good for food, and that it was a delight to the eyes, and that the tree was to be desired to make one wise, she took of its fruit and ate..." (Gen. 3:6). Again, the sin was first conceived in the thought-life of Eve – she admired the outward appearance of the fruit and desired to eat it in order to be wise. The result of wrong thinking was the commission of an external sin – she ate and gave to her husband to eat also. The thought-world, the heart and mind, is the first arena and so the first cause of the external act. Thought gave birth to action. It produces something that did not previously exist and in this case ought never to have existed. In the Garden of Eden, Adam and Eve made a choice first in their thought-life and this ill-advised choice produced an immoral act – sin resulted. An individual's conduct is intimately linked with his thought-life. The two are inseparably linked. We must therefore conclude that the pattern of the Christian's conduct can be spiritual only by training the mind and heart to be in harmony with God's will and purpose for life. Christianity is a permanent mental and psychological commitment.

We emphasize again that our outward actions are the inevitable results of our inward thoughts. But we must not think that our thought-life only produces negative actions and results. Nothing is further from the truth. We have already shown that the inspired writer informs us that as a man thinks in his heart, so is he (cf. Prov. 23:7, KJV). This being true, if an individual thinks good and wholesome thoughts, he will just as inevitably produce good and virtuous results. This is actualized in the creation: God thought, God spoke, and it came into being. This is not to say that the world is just a thought-world, as the Christian Scientists are prone to believe and so teach. Nor is the world merely an extension of God's essence, as the Eastern mystical religions aver. The world is a real, external reality outside of God because God created it outside of himself. God thought and spoke, and the world came into being quite apart from and totally outside of his own person. The important thing here, however, is that God first had the creation proposed within his thought-life. The universe and all that comprises it first existed in the mind of God and so was in God's thought-life before he brought it into actual existence.

If the creation, the external universe, is the result of God's thought, then it reveals and exhibits who and what God is. The universe and all that it entails are in one sense at least, revelations of God: "And God saw everything that he had made, and behold, it was very good" (Gen. 1:31). God first gave thought to it and then he brought forth the external world which was described by him at the conclusion of the creative process as being "very good." Thus, God's thinking exhibits what he truly is – God is "very good." In much the same manner, our acts in the external world about us spring forth from our thought-life and exhibit the quality of our inner character. While we cannot create out of nothing, as did God, we can create as God did. We are able, by our thought-life, to bring good into existence in the world. We can actually "create" in some limited measure as God created. Granted, we are finite and quite limited and therefore cannot create "out of nothing," but nevertheless, understanding these limitations and differences, it is perfectly proper to say that we can create as God creates. We can bring forth good and not evil in this world.

From this we determine that human spirituality and creativity always begins inside our thought-world, inside our hearts and minds. But the truth of the matter is that we can also potentially be a death-producing source in the world if we yield our thought-life over to the proclivities of the wrong power. If we become disciples of self, or of pride, or of Satan, we will bring forth the fruits of the world. On the other hand, if we give our thought-life over to the Spirit of Christ, the fruit of the resurrected and glorified Lord will flow through us into the external world. If our minds are grounded in his noble and lofty thoughts, then our bodies will tend to work out the fruit of such thoughts in our everyday lives. The results of such are that the world will become a much better place in which to live. Little by little our lives will radiate beneficial things into the lives of others until the same noble and lofty thoughts are firmly planted within the hearts and lives of others. Therefore, what we think that is wholesome and good becomes extremely important and extraordinarily essential in our world. What we think that is positive and salutary will determine the way in which our society will move. No wonder Paul's uplifting words in his Philippian letter are so advantageous if they are put into application in our lives.

> Finally, brethren, whatever is true, whatever is honorable, whatever is just, whatever is pure, whatever is lovely, whatever is gracious, if there is any excellence, if there is anything worthy of praise, think about these things. What you have learned and received and heard and seen in me, do; and the God of peace will be with you (Phil. 4:8-9).

Paul admonishes us here to focus our thoughts on the things that belong to a Christ-like life. If we do, a transformation will take place, not only in us, but in the lives of others around us. We become like Christ; others around us will often tend also to become more like Christ; the end result being that the evil is pushed steadily out of our lives and the good is brought ever more conspicuously to the forefront.

How powerful and sobering is the thought that I can bring forth, out of my thought-life and into the world, either that which leads to life, or that which produces death. And this power not only affects my life, but it also infiltrates and affects the lives of those with whom I come in contact. Man's thought-life is the most unique thing about him, and thus the one thing that distinguishes him from all the rest of the creation. Man's thought-life is what he ultimately is and his calling in life is to utilize this thought-life to love God with all his internal power – his heart, his soul, his mind – and to love his neighbor as he loves himself. Being free from the bonds of sin and the results of this benighted slavery can be a reality to us only when we learn in the face of temptation to control and use the power of our thought-life to beneficial ends. The spiritual battles that we fight will be won or lost in our thought-life. Our quest for spiritual maturity will be successful or unsuccessful depending upon our thought-life. Thus, the greatest battle that we ever face in life is fought, first and foremost, in the world of thought. So, how very appropriate is Paul's admonition that we "take every thought captive to obey Christ" (2 Cor. 10:5b). How very true is the proverb, "As a man thinketh in his heart, so is he" (Prov. 23:7; KJV).

In summation, the manner in which we think is the supremely important thing about our spiritual life. What we think will determine whether we ultimately become a spiritually mature Christian or a spiritually weak Christian. The greatest challenge before us, therefore, is to develop a godly thought-life which results in a proper spiritual life. Let us fill our minds with good things, with God's love, purity, discipline, and the host of other God-like virtues. If we intensely and earnestly cherish godly thoughts and ideals, we will one day realize them in our lives. What we think about, we become. And as we become like this ourselves, very often so will those individuals in whose lives we make an impact – those whom we care about the most. We must so live. Our future as well as the future of our world depends on this.

Discussion Questions

1. The battle in quest for personal spiritual maturity must first begin in the individual's heart and mind. Explain. _____

_____

_____

2. How have you experienced the following truth in your life? An individual's conduct in life, expressed in deeds and actions, is first of all an expression of his or her thought-life. _____

_____

_____

3. In our thought-life we can emulate God's creation process. How?_____

_____

_____

XIII. Freedom from Sin's Consequences – Separation

What am I as a man? It seems that man has always been his own most vexing problem. How are we to think of ourselves? Does not every affirmation we make concerning ourselves – our stature, our virtue, our place in the universe – involve us in contradictions when fully analyzed? What am I as man? The inspired writer describes man in these beautiful words:

> What is man that thou art mindful of him or the son of man, that thou carest for him? Thou didst make him for a little while lower than the angels, thou hast crowned him with glory and honor, putting everything in subjection under his feet (Hebrews 2:6-8).

We are a little lower than the angels. We are the glory of the creation, but at the same time we are often the very worst of creation. This is one of the vexing problems that we face as human beings. What is really involved in being a part of humanity, and especially a part of the Christian element of humanity?

The simplest answer to the question as to what we are is probably best represented by this offering: we are, we exist, and we exist as rational and moral beings. This means that we are like God on one level, and we are like God's creation in another. We have a relationship to God, but also to all that God has created for us in the world. We are separated from God because God is infinite, but we are like God in that we are created in his image. In our finiteness we are like the animals, the plants, and the material things of the physical world. On the other hand, we are also separate from these finite things because we are personal and sentient but they are not.

So it all comes down to the point of recognizing that man's center of existence is positioned somewhere between God and the impersonal, finite creation. Man is a child of nature, subject to its fluctuations, compelled by its necessities, driven by its impulses, and confined within the brevity of its finite years. Man is also a spiritual, personal being who stands uniquely outside of nature, life, himself, his reason, and the world. He is in a position of dominion over nature and is charged by God with the responsibility to nurture and care for it. This freedom to rule over nature and its lack of dominion over him reveals the image of God in man. It reveals also that we have a responsibility to God and that God expects from us to be answerable and accountable as to how we have conducted ourselves as covenant partners in his creation. Man's situation in the scheme of things may be diagrammed as shown in figure 1.

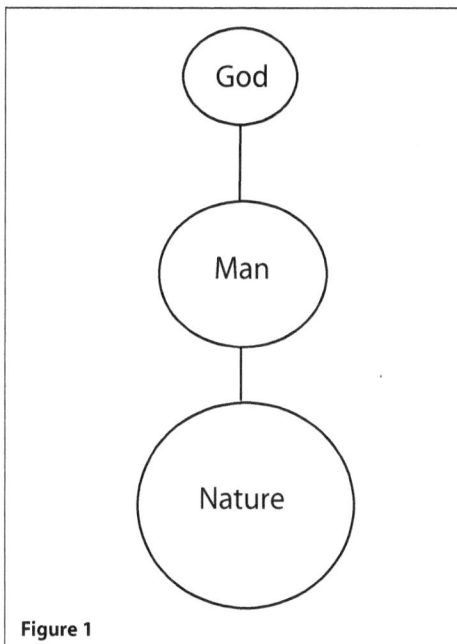

Figure 1

The major problems which man has faced in life have been caused primarily by his rebellion in trying to operate outside the circle in which God meant for him to exist. Man is always trying to become what he is not, both in an elevating sense and in a devaluing sense. This condition is always indicative of surly human pride and the result of sin. For example: man wanted to become like God, so he ate of the forbidden fruit in the Garden of Eden (cf. Genesis 3). Man pretends that he is not limited. He assumes that by some means or other he can gradually transcend his finite limitations until he becomes equal to or even identical with God. The sin that is at the heart of this rebellion is pride, and it shows its presence in not wanting to be what God wants him to be, but desiring to be dependent on self and independent of God. The essence of human sinfulness is, then, in the refusal to accept the limits of human existence. Man, in his freedom, wants to be more like God and so falls from a state of fellowship with the Lord through arrogance.

On the other hand, man tries to think of himself as a totally rational being. Man was created with the ability to reason and many times he misuses this God-given ability. He refuses to bow to God and acknowledge him as Creator. With such a rationalistic concept, man ends up taking a blind leap into the dark where he is continually embarrassed and torn within himself because his own rationality demands an answer as to who he is and why he exists. As we have stated before, man must be a rational being in order to have fellowship with God. It is this ability to reason and this superior intellect that makes it possible for God in his grace to grant man some vestige of knowledge about himself:

> May grace and peace be multiplied to you in the *knowledge* of God and Jesus Christ. His divine power has granted to us all things that pertain to life and godliness, through the *knowledge* of him who called us…. For if, after they have escaped the defilements of the world through the *knowledge* of our Lord and Savior Jesus Christ….But grow in the grace and *knowledge* of our Lord and Savior Jesus Christ (2 Peter 1:2-3; 2:20; 3:18).

Yet man must not misuse this rational attribute, for as reason and intellect are entailed in making man in the "image of God," they also make possible troubling character traits like self-will and pride, which involve sin. So, sin presupposes rationality and voluntary decision.

Man does not have within him the potential to be God, cannot be infinite in action, and cannot be truly free in any part of life, so in his foolish rebellion he falls to the ground crushed when he tries to be God. In his mutinous ways he is divided from God and damned by what he has become. By desiring to be God, yet not having within himself the possibility of being God because he is finite, man is errantly divided and separated in his twisted rationality, his perverse morality, his arrogant thought-life, his undisciplined action, and his depraved feelings. And on the other hand, because he is still in some sense made in the image of God, man cannot be a part of God's non-rational creation – the animal or the natural world – either. Being created in the image and glory of God, man cannot find a place of rest and peaceful existence in the animal or natural world. Man may try to live like an animal, may become depraved as were the Romans whom Paul discussed and described in Romans 1, but in such a state he finds no rest either. He is ripped apart by those inner emotions and feelings which were not given to the rest of God's creation. Man cannot hide himself among the animals or in the natural world, for like it or not he always bears the marks of the image of God. There is no peace, no contentment, or quality of life for man so long as he continues to strive to live outside the circle of existence God has planned for him. When he tries to elevate himself to the level of God, he continuously fails. When he tries to lower himself to the level of the animal world, he also fails. His only hope is to live, move, and have his existence in the sphere in which God in his infallible wisdom has placed him.

An illustration of the irritating frustrations involved in such inner turmoil and quiet desperation in man's life is found in the life of Sigmund Freud and his fiancée. Freud did not believe in the concept of love. His philosophy was that the end of all things is physical – specifically, sex! Yet, even though he did not know it, Freud needed love, for he was created with this need as an element intrinsic to his psyche. He was, just like Adam, incomplete without the love of another human being. He was created in the image of God, whether he liked it or not, and whether he admitted it or not. So Freud wrote to his fiancée, "When you come to me, little Princess, love me *irrationally*." As hard as he may have tried, Freud was prevented from living his rational, non-personal existence for he had been created with that personal, emotional need of real love, for he was made in the image of God. If man tries to substitute himself for God, or if he denies God, then in the end he is an incomplete being, living less than a whole life.

The individual who chooses to leave the circle of existence that God has planned for him finds himself divided and inwardly separated at every turn. He is confused and frustrated at every point of the compass simply by what God made him. Every part of his nature shouts, "I am man!" No matter how great the distance man may try to put between himself and the sphere God intended for him to live in, there will always be the conflicted inward voices that cry out from every part of his exasperated nature: "I am man; I am man!"

Whenever man, in his rebellion against God, decides to leave his sphere of existence, he has two possibilities: he can strive to be his own god, or he can become like some inferior being. The fact of the matter is that man cannot be God so he must either revert back to his proper sphere by simply being a man, or else he lives out his days in a lower order of life. Furthermore, it is always true that the individual who chooses not to remain in the circle of existence made for him by God will find a place for himself somewhere in a lower circle of existence. Paul addresses such individuals with these descriptive words: "They are darkened in their understanding, alienated from the life of God because of the ignorance that is in them, due to their hardness of heart; they have become callous and have given themselves up to licentiousness, greedy to practice every kind of uncleanness" (Eph. 4:18-19). A life that is not attuned to God's will and purpose can never realize the full potential of life that God has planned for those who humbly and obediently serve him.

History has demonstrated repeatedly that human nature seems to possess a constant tendency to retrogress and degenerate toward a lower level of life. In his desire to stretch his muscles in the direction of self-assertion and independence, man always falls painfully and embarrassingly on his face. But even in this lower existence, man finds separation rather than wholeness. Man in sin is not only alienated from God, but he is also disengaged from his fellow man and nature. This is vividly illustrated in the story of the fall of man in Genesis 3. Due to anger and jealousy, Cain killed Abel and created a state of hostility and separation between man and his fellow. This unfortunate situation was in addition to the alienation resulting from the fall of Adam and Eve. God's curse pronounced upon the sin of Adam and Eve brought about a state of separation from self and nature: "To the woman [God] said, 'I will greatly multiply your pain in childbearing; in pain you shall bring forth children, yet your desire shall be for your husband, and he shall rule over you" (vs. 16). Here we see the horrible fruits of disobedience as it ended in separation from self and man.

> "And to Adam [God] said, 'Because you have listened to the voice of your wife, and have eaten of the tree of which I commanded you, "You shall not eat it," cursed is the ground because of you; in toil you shall eat of it all the days of your life; thorns and thistles it shall bring forth to you; and you shall eat the plants of the field. In the sweat of

your face you shall eat bread till you return to the ground, for out of it you were taken; you are dust, and to dust you shall return'" (Gen. 3:17-19).

Thus, the sin committed by the original pair in Eden resulted in man's separation from nature, self, and God. It is impossible for faithless and mutinous man to remain in the state for which he was created – in harmony with God's creation and in fellowship with his Creator - because sin is by its very nature and in its essence incompatible with both harmony and fellowship. Man in sin caused all of these separations, none of them existed prior to the entrance of human rebellion into the created order: separations between man and God, between man and himself, between man and man, and between man and nature. Because of sin, man has lost all of his best potential, what he could be and what he could enjoy. In every area of life and relationship, sin has robbed him of what he could be if he had only remained in his proper place.

Thus, sin becomes a fateful and tragic habitus leading men at last down the road to total destruction. Sin begets more and greater sin, and in its wake comes greater separation. In addition, the sin of one individual involves everyone and everything associated with him through its poisonous and caustic influence. A sin in the sphere of thought leads to transgressions in word and action. In short, the whole life, the whole being of man thereby becomes sinful and corrupt. And because man is a part of his culture and, in fact, is the builder of his culture, his sin affects at least in some sense all of those with whom he comes in contact. And because sin is rooted within the human heart, no activity – social, political, or spiritual – is exempt from its destructive influence. The result of sin is not just estrangement from God, although this is indeed its most shattering consequence, but also from man and all creation. When man is living in accordance with his original purpose as the image of God, however unerringly, he is in harmony with God, man, and creation.

It is into this situation of man's separation from God, himself, man, and nature that the modern non-Christian psychologists and psychiatrists have entered the picture with their unsatisfactory attempts at bringing unity into the life of unredeemed man. These professionals, as well intentioned as most are, are nevertheless doomed to failure because their solutions are grounded neither in God, nor in man's deep-seated need for God. Man has always been and will always be a worshipping being. He will in every age, no matter how sophisticated, seek to worship something or someone greater than himself, for man is "incurably religious." Augustine put it very well when he said, "Thou hast made us for Thyself and our souls are restless until they rest in thee."

This vertical dimension of man's need for God means that the human spirit requires a meaningful relationship with its Creator and all creation in order to possess that wholeness of life which every human being seeks. Yet many non-Christian psychologists and psychiatrists in their own rebellion against the Deity deny this fundamental need of the human psyche. Much of modern psychology and psychiatry is grounded in the fundamentals of Freudian theory and therapy. Freud, who called himself "a completely godless Jew," taught that religion belongs to the infancy of the race. To his way of thinking, religion was invented to fulfill man's childish need and when one comes of age, he no longer needs religion. He further believed that man has no need for faith or any sort of redeemer figure, for man is not responsible for his sin. Man is neither responsible for evil nor accountable for good because all behavior is caused not by man, but by conditions before and around him. Vast numbers of technical studies and a mountain of evidence reveal to the contrary, that Freudian principles do not in fact work and that Freudian psychiatry and psychology has, by and large, proven ineffective.[1] So it is evident that one cannot turn in the direction of Freudian psychology and psychiatry to find unity in life and freedom from inward and outward separation that man so desires.

In what direction, then, do we turn to avoid the brokenness and alienation that is so evident in the life of contemporary man? It may seem simplistic to some of us to say so, but the way to turn for relief is back to our very source of life – God! This turning back does not necessarily mean that we will put an end to all separation that has become a part of fallen humanity. We will not end all sense of separation, for this is the result of sin in our lives and in the world around us and even though God has wrought a mighty work of redemption

---

[1] Jay E. Adams. *Competent to Counsel*. Grand Rapids: Baker Book House, 1970.

through the sacrifice of his sinless Son, the fact yet remains that all men are sinners (cf. Rom. 3:23). It does mean, however, that through Christ Jesus we can overcome most of the psychological and spiritual effects of this painful separation. We don't have to harbor guilt feelings and the sense of being cut off from our Creator, our fellow man, and the world of nature. We can never achieve moral, physical, or psychological perfection in this life, but in Christ there can be a substantial overcoming and conquering of these troublesome problems and a much greater wholeness of life than we could ever experience outside of his fellowship and counsel. We will undoubtedly face future problems and psychological hang-ups, even occasionally a few guilt feelings, but if we strive to remain in harmony with God's will and purpose for our lives, we will recognize that we are not entirely on our own. We do not have to depend on self and that alone. We are living before an infinite-personal God who knows us intimately and is fully aware of what we are striving to become in Christ. With this knowledge and the comfort of his ongoing fellowship, we can, even in the midst of the awful miseries in this world and the frequent sense of separation that is so much a part of the existence of fallen man, have real freedom from the bonds of sin and peace "that passes understanding."

Kenneth S. Kantzer in his short synopsis sums up well the true nature of man; would that we could come to have some genuine sense of it through a progressive spiritual maturity as we await in hope that better place where "the curse" is no more (Rev. 22:3):

> The Christian revelation at its center points to the doctrine of creation, according to which man was "made a little lower than God" (Heb. 8:5), crown of the entire creative process (Gen. 1:26; 2:3), declared "very good" by God himself, entrusted with possession of the earth (Gen. 1:31), instructed to rule over earthly creatures (Gen. 1:36; Psa. 8), and commanded to subdue earth and its resources for human well being (cf. Gen. 1:28-30)....In Sum, by contrast with the rest of earth's creation, man was made to be godlike (Gen. 1:26-27) for personal companionship with God (Gen. 3:8).[1]

Discussion Questions

1. How is humanity like God, yet at the same time, like God's cre-

---

[1] Kenneth S. Kantzer. "Doctrine of Man," *Baker's Dictionary of Christian Ethics*. Grand Rapids: Baker Book House, 1970, p. 403.

ated beings? What problems has this caused for humanity? __

_____

_____

2. What does Augustine's famous prayer to God, "Thou hast made us for Thyself and our souls are restless until they rest in Thee," mean in our relationship with God?_____

_____

_____

_____

Index of Biblical Passages

Bibliography

Works Cited and Recommended

Adams, Jay E. *Competent to Counsel*. Grand Rapids: Baker Book-House, 1970.

Allen, James. *As A Man Thinketh*, quoted from Baxter's Sermons, No.449, January 9, 1966.

Bonhoeffer, Dietrich. *The Cost of Discipleship*. New York: The Mac-Millian Company, 1946.

Brunner, Frederick Dale. *A Theology of the Holy Spirit*. Grand Rapids:Eerdmans Publishers, 1973.

Chardin, Teilhard de. *Le Milieu Divin*. London: Collins, 1960.

Chittister, Joan. *Wisdom Distilled from the Daily*. San Francisco: 1st Harper Collins, 1991.

Colson, Charles W. *Born Again*. Old Tappan, N.J.: Fleming H. Revell-Company, 1977.

Davies, W. R. *Down Peacock's Feathers*. New York: The MacMillian-Company, 1946.

Kantzer, Kenneth S. "Doctrine of Man," *Baker's Dictionary of Christian Ethics*. Grand Rapids: Baker Book House, 1973.

Lewis, C. S. *Mere Christianity*. New York: The MacMillian Company,1971.

Macquarrie, John. *Paths in Spirituality*. New York: Harper & Row,1972.

Muller-Fahrenholz, Geiko. *God's Spirit: Transforming a World in Crisis*. New York: The Continuum Publishing Company, 1995.

Richards, Lawrence O. *A Practical Theology of Spirituality*. Grand Rapids: Zondervan Publishing House, 1987.

Roberts, Robert C. *The Strengths of a Christian*. Philadelphia: TheWestminster Press, 1984.

Schweitzer, Albert. *The Quest for the Historical Jesus*. London: A. C.Black, Ltd., 1910.

Shakespeare, William. *Henry VI*, Part II, Sc. 1.20.

Stewart, James S. *A Man in Christ*. New York: Harper & Brothers, n.d.

Taylor, Richard Shelley. *The Disciplined Life*. Minneapolis: Dimen-sionBooks, 1962.

White, James Emery. *A Mind for God*. Downers Grove, IL: InterVarsi-tyPress, 2006.

www.ingramcontent.com/pod-product-compliance
Lightning Source LLC
LaVergne TN
LVHW021447080426
835509LV00018B/2186